making disciples of oral learners

To proclaim His story
where it has not been known before…

ION / LCWE

Originally Published as
Lausanne Occasional Paper (LOP) No. 54
"Making Disciples of Oral Learners"
Issues Group No. 25

Avery Willis – Convener, Steve Evans – Co-Convener

Lausanne Committee for World Evangelization
2004 Forum for World Evangelization
Pattya, Thailand
September 29 to October 5, 2004

Editorial Committee:
Samuel Chiang
Steve Evans
Annette Hall
Grant Lovejoy, chair
David Payne
Sheila Ponraj
Mark Snowden
Avery Willis

The list of all Issues Group No. 25 participants and contributors to this paper appears at
the end of this edition.

Series Editor for the 2004 Forum LOPs (commencing with no. 30): David Claydon.
In encouraging the publication and study of the Occasional Papers, the Lausanne
Committee or World Evangelization does not necessarily endorse every viewpoint
expressed in these papers.

This edition published by International Orality Network

To proclaim His story where it has not been known before (re: Rom. 15:20)

Photos: Langfia Ayeona, Taitiana Cardeal, Steve Evans
Book and Jacket Design: Mike Mirabella

ISBN 0-9772089-1-5

Printed at SUDHINDRA Offset Process, Bangalore, INDIA
info@sudhindraprint.com

 # Contents

1

growing awareness of a global situation

Growing Awareness
of a Global Situation

P ASTOR Dinanath of India tells his story of ministry among
his people:[1]

I was saved from a Hindu family in 1995 through
a cross-cultural missionary. I had a desire to learn
more about the word of God and I shared this with the
missionary. The missionary sent me to Bible College
in 1996. I finished my two years of theological study
and came back to my village in 1998. I started sharing
the good news in the way as I learnt in the Bible
College. To my surprise my people were not able to
understand my message. A few people accepted the
Lord after much labour. I continued to preach the
gospel, but there were little results. I was discouraged
and confused and did not know what to do.

But then Pastor Dinanath's story takes a major turn:

In 1999 I attended a seminar where I learnt how to
communicate the gospel using different oral methods.
I understood the problem in my communication as I
was mostly using a lecture method with printed books,

---

1   The account from Pastor Dinanath is provided by S. D. Ponraj and Sheila Ponraj.

which I learnt in the Bible school. After the seminar I went to the village but this time I changed my way of communication. I started using a storytelling method in my native language. I used gospel songs and the traditional music of my people. This time the people in the villages began to understand the gospel in a better way. As a result of it people began to come in large numbers. Many accepted Christ and took baptism. There was one church with few baptized members in 1999 when I attended the seminar. But now in 2004, in six years we have 75 churches with 1350 baptized members and 100 more people are ready for baptism.

The account described in the first part of Pastor Dinanath's story is not an isolated instance. The gospel is being proclaimed now to more people than at any other time in history, yet many of those are not really *hearing* it. Unfortunately, most evangelical leaders do not realize the magnitude of the problem. Those affected by it include the 4 billion oral communicators of the world: people who can't, don't, or won't take in new information or communicate by literate means. Oral communicators are found in every cultural group in the world and they constitute approximately two-thirds of the world's population! Yet we are not communicating the gospel effectively with them. We will not succeed in reaching the majority of the world unless we make some crucial changes.

Ironically, an estimated 90% of the world's Christian workers presenting the gospel use highly literate communication styles. They use the printed page or expositional, analytical and logical presentations of God's word. This makes it difficult, if not impossible, for oral learners to hear and understand the message and communicate it to others. As the ones bringing the message, it is our responsibility to communicate our message in their terms. The pages that follow are intended to help point the way for us to do that.

Current estimates indicate that around two-thirds of the world's population are oral communicators either by necessity or by choice. To effectively communicate with them, we must defer to their oral communication style. Our presentations must match their oral learning styles and preferences. Instead of using outlines, lists, steps and principles we need to use culturally relevant approaches they would understand. Are we willing to seek God to become better stewards of the Great Commission and address these issues in serving Him in these last days? The Lausanne Forum of 2004 has responded to this challenge in the form of the Issue Group focused on "Making Disciples of Oral Learners."

This terminology, "making disciples" and "oral learners," is a mix of the familiar and unfamiliar. By "making disciples" we mean enabling people to respond in faith to Jesus Christ and to grow in relationship with Him and others with the goal of obeying everything that Jesus commanded (Mt. 28:20). Or as Paul described it in more detail, making disciples involves bringing people to be

> ...filled with the knowledge of [God's] will in all spiritual wisdom and understanding, so that [they] will walk in a manner worthy of the Lord, to please Him in all respects, bearing fruit in every good work and increasing in the knowledge of God; strengthened with all power, according to His glorious might, for the attaining of all steadfastness and patience; joyously giving thanks to the Father, who has qualified us to share in the inheritance of the saints in light" (Col. 1:9b-12, NASB).

Normally discipling takes place in the context of churches that make disciples and plant other churches. By "oral learners" we mean those people who learn best and whose lives are most likely to be transformed when instruction comes in oral forms. Many groups transmit their beliefs, heritage, values and other important

information by means of stories, proverbs, poetry, chants, music, dances, ceremonies and rites of passage. The spoken, sung, or chanted word associated with these activities often consists of ornate and elaborate ways to communicate. Those who use these art forms well are highly regarded among their people. Cultures which use these forms of communication are sometimes called "oral cultures."

The members of these societies are referred to as "oral learners" or "oral communicators." In this discussion, we use the terms "oral learner" and "oral communicator" interchangeably at times. With the phrase oral "learner" the focus is more on the receiving act—hearing an oral communication. With the phrase oral "communicator" the focus is more on the act of telling. These societies are relational, group-oriented, face-to-face cultures. Most of the members of these societies learn best through aural means.

Those who have grown up in highly literate societies tend to think of literacy as the norm and oral communication as a deviation. That is not so. All societies, including those having a highly literate segment, have oral communication at their core. Oral communication is the basic function on which writing and literacy is based. When literacy persists in a culture for generations, it begins to change the way people think, act and communicate—so much so that the members of that literate society may not even realize how their communication styles are different from those of the majority of the world who are oral communicators. These members of a literate society then tend to communicate the gospel in the literate style that speaks to them.

But oral learners find it difficult to follow literate-styled presentations, even if they are made orally. It is not enough to take materials created for literates and simply read them onto a recorded format. Making something audible does not necessarily make it an "oral" style of communication. Not everything on a CD or audiotape is "oral." Some of it is clearly literate in its style even though it is spoken or audible. The same thing is true of other media products created for literate audiences. They may have literate stylistic features that confuse oral learners.

Some people are oral learners because of their limited education. They may not read or write at all, or they may read with difficulty. Many oral learners can read but prefer learning by oral means. If their culture is traditionally oral, they frequently prefer to learn through oral methods even if they are highly educated. When many people in a culture are oral learners, it affects the whole culture and permeates many aspects of people's lives, such as thought processes and decision-making. Scholars call this whole cluster of characteristics and effects "orality." The Deaf community displays many of these traits that scholars associate with the term orality, though the Deaf cannot properly be called "oral."[2] Likewise, there are literates who demonstrate many characteristics associated with the concept of orality, an effect referred to as "secondary orality." (*Secondary orality* will be addressed in detail in chapter six.)

In summary, approximately two-thirds of the world's population lives by orality. Many of them have no other choice because they have inadequate literacy skills, but others who are quite literate strongly prefer to learn via oral means. Together they comprise an oral majority who cannot or will not learn well through print-based instruction. This poses a challenge to those who want to communicate effectively with them.

After listening to a speaker discuss the challenge that orality poses, a ministry leader approached the speaker. "If what you say is true," he told the speaker, "we will have to rethink everything we are doing." He was right. Taking orality seriously can revolutionize ministries—and has the potential to greatly increase our effectiveness. But what should we do differently? The following chapters describe specific ways to improve effectiveness in making disciples of oral learners. They describe practical steps that various churches, organizations and agencies are taking. A number of them share a common vision that addresses the predominance of oral communicators in the world. That common vision is:

---

2   Deaf with an upper case "D" by common practice refers to the people group or population segment, in contrast to lower case "deaf" referring to the physical characteristic.

- God's word for every "tribe, tongue, people and nation";
- addressing the issue of orality;
- resulting in church planting movements;
- providing resources for oral, chronological, narrative presentations of God's word, in order to disciple and equip leaders.

To these issues we now turn.

2

God's Word
for the
whole

world

God's Word
for the Whole World

WHAT is the hope of reaching the four billion persons who are oral learners? What is the hope for getting God's word to the speakers of the four thousand languages still without His word?[3]

The answer comes from Jesus' own model: "...with many similar parables Jesus spoke the word to them, *as much as they could understand*" (Mk. 4:33 NIV, emphasis added). In fact, the passage goes on to say: "He did not say anything to them without using a parable" (Mk. 4:34a NIV). Jesus chose his teaching style to match his listeners' capacities. So should we. Jesus used familiar oral means that they understood. So can we.

One straightforward way to communicate to oral learners in a way they will understand is for them to hear the stories of the Bible in an oral, sequential pattern that they can absorb and remember. The communication of stories in this way has come to be referred to as "chronological Bible storying." It is a proclamation of God's word in a culturally relevant way that oral

---

3   Statistics as of Sep. 30, 2004 from Wycliffe International indicate 4558 languages without any of the Bible, out of the 6913 languages currently spoken in the world (see *Ethnologue*, 15th ed.). Dec. 31, 2003 statistics from the United Bible Societies indicate only 2355 languages have some or all of the Bible. Of these, only 414 have an adequate Bible, 1068 have an adequate New Testament, and 873 have at least one book of the Bible (see http://www.biblesociety.org/latestnews/latest273-slr2003stats.html).

learners can understand and respond to.

A "storying" approach to ministry involves selecting and crafting stories that convey the essential biblical message, in a way that is sensitive to the worldview of the receptor society. The stories are faithful to the biblical text, and at the same time told in a natural, compelling manner in the heart language. They are expressed in the manner in which that society conveys a treasured, true story. The process also is done in a way that facilitates the hearers in processing the story in a culturally relevant way—normally involving some sort of discussion about or interaction with the story.

Without the presence of God's word there will be no true spiritual movements. Without God's word, an incipient movement will ultimately collapse, splinter, fall prey to cults, or face syncretism with existing local beliefs and practices. Unbelievers need Christians to provide His word in culturally appropriate formats in order for them to understand it and respond to it, but understanding and responding is still not enough for a spiritual movement. Those who respond need to be able to reproduce it—to share it themselves with others who can, in turn, share it with others, with this pattern being repeated many times over. A spiritual movement of this sort can provide a foundation for faith, witness, and church life. For this to happen in an oral society and involve the majority of those oral communicators who will likely remain oral communicators for their lifetime, the process will have to be an oral one for evangelism, discipleship, leader training and church planting. Because of the communication and learning styles of oral communicators, reflecting their thought and decision-making processes, this should be primarily through narrative presentations of God's word.

This does not mean that we discourage literacy or neglect literates. Experience shows that once oral learners accept the gospel, some will have the desire and persistence to become literate in order to read the Bible for themselves. The development of oral strategies is not a deterrent to translating the Bible into every language. In fact, the opposite is true. These burgeoning church planting movements that result from an oral proclamation will need the whole counsel of God. Requiring non-Christians to learn to read just so that they can consider the Christian faith puts unnecessary obstacles in their path.

We wish all peoples had the written translation of the Scripture in their heart language. But, for the illiterate, written Scripture is not accessible even if it is available in their own language. On the other hand, a Bible translation program that begins with the oral presentation of the Bible through storying and continues with a translation and literacy program is the most comprehensive strategy for communicating the word of God in their heart language. It offers a viable possibility of making disciples of oral learners while at the same time providing the whole counsel of God.

We do not want our call for oral approaches to be seen as setting oral and literate approaches in opposition to one another. It is not a matter of "either-or," but "both-and." Again, the Bible itself gives the model. There are examples throughout the Scriptures where both the written word of God and the spoken word of God are given prominence, often side by side. For example, Moses wrote down the words of the Law (Deut. 31-33). God instructed him to write the words down in a song. God also instructed him to teach the song to the Israelites so that they would always have it in their hearts and on their lips and always remember it.

Similarly in today's world, we envision a systemic approach to evangelism, discipleship, church planting and leadership development that can involve oral, audio, audio-visual media and print. A systemic, sequential approach with a society of largely oral communicators, for example, might begin with oral Bible storying. It could then possibly begin to involve audio and radio presentations of these same oral stories and other audio and radio products of a broader array based on translated biblical material.[4] In some cases primary visual products may

---

4   Examples of some of these sorts of audio and radio presentations in vernacular languages include Global Recordings Network's various Scripture resources; the *JESUS Film* audio versions; *Lives of the Prophets*, *Life of Jesus* and *Lives of the Apostles* audio versions; Faith Comes by Hearing dramatized recordings of the New Testament; and the Radio Bible, which consists of 365 fifteen-minute broadcasts of stories from the Old and New Testaments. These are described in the Resources section.

be produced and effectively used.[5] Then the process in some situations may move on to the preparation and distribution of audio-visual products based on translation of further biblical material.[6] Throughout the approach the undergirding process of Bible translation, at first orally and then in a literate manner, provides the entire counsel of God.

In a sequential approach like this, the first biblical stories we use focus very intently on the unique cultural perspective of the people. Specificity to that culture is crucial in order for them to understand the gospel well and embrace Christ. The same will be true of the stories we use in initial discipleship. Later stages in the strategy will give them ever-larger portions of the Bible; at that point our focus will have shifted from cultural specificity to providing complete books of the Bible, a New Testament and finally the whole Bible.

God's word has transforming impact on people's lives when we present it in ways that they can understand it. For example, missionaries worked for twenty-five years with the Tiv tribe in central Nigeria and saw only twenty-five baptized believers as a result.[7] That is an average of one believer per year of ministry. Their medium of communication was preaching, which they had learned in Bible school was the proper way to evangelize.

Then some young Tiv Christians set the gospel story to musical chants, the indigenous medium of communication. Almost immediately the gospel began to spread like wildfire

---

5   Examples of primary visual products can include print illustrations and booklets depicting scenes from Bible stories and products like Deaf Missions visual recordings.
6   Examples of audio-visual products are the *JESUS Film* and related Genesis and Luke videos; *God's Story;* and *The Hope.*
7   This story is taken from C. Peter Wagner, *Strategies for Church Growth* (Ventura, California: Regal Books, 1987), 91-92.

and soon a quarter million Tivs were worshipping Jesus. The Tivs were not as resistant as the missionaries had thought. A change in method brought abundant fruit. Prior to this the gospel had been "proclaimed," but it had not been heard! The communication strategy chosen had not spoken to the heart of the people. This story underscores that groups may not be necessarily unresponsive, but have not yet received the gospel in their learning style. Where traditional literate methods have failed to reach people, appropriate oral strategies have succeeded.

When Christian workers follow these principles, non-Christians are more likely to give the gospel a hearing, more likely to respond in faith to it, and more likely to spread it enthusiastically to their friends, relatives and neighbours. In the Togolese town of Kpele-Dafo, for instance, the hamlet sprang to life when the message came: "The storyteller is coming!"[8] The sound of drumming announced the coming of the storyteller. Men left their game of *adí*, tailors closed shop, and yawning children roused themselves. The drumming intensified as the storyteller took his place in the center of the village, where he seated himself on a low, carved bench. The elders of the village arrived in their finery and the animated storyteller, Antoine, exchanged ritual, formalized greetings with his audience. The fetish priestess, clothed in white and wearing her horsehair amulet, stood near, watching intensely.

As night fell and the logs crackled in the fire, Antoine began in melodic, poetic style: "*In the beginning, God created the heavens and the earth...*" When he reached the repeated phrase, "*And God saw that it was good,*" he sang a song composed in their familiar call and response style. He sang a line about God's

---

8   This story is from Carla Bowman, *Communications Bridges to Oral Cultures* (Tucson AZ, Scriptures In Use, 2004).

creative work and the villagers sang back, "*And God saw that it was good.*" The villagers quickly memorized their part and sang it enthusiastically. Before long, the villagers began dancing too, to express their delight at this God who created a good world. The village headman joined in the dance, signaling his approval of the story and the event. Antoine continued his story long into the night, accompanied by the sound of drumming and joined in his song by the villagers. When the fire had burned low and the story-song finally ended, no one wanted to leave. The whole experience had engulfed them. A new truth was dawning and their world would never be the same.

Antoine returned many times over the next several weeks, bringing story after story in this way—stories about Abraham and his sons, about the other prophets, about Jesus and God's community. These stories spoke to the villagers' longings, needs and practices, prompting long conversations with Antoine and among themselves. Gently but firmly the Holy Spirit used the stories to do his transforming work. In time extended families made God's story their own story, the God of the Bible their God. A fetish priest burned his amulets, talismans and jujus because he no longer needed their protection.

The same storytelling approach was used to bring about the surrender of strongholds and for discipleship. Through Bible storytelling the word of God came to life in the African context. The biblical stories continued as the people of Kpele-Dafo grew in their newfound faith, meeting in house churches and taking this message to neighboring villages. The same process has now taken place throughout the Volta region of Togo, Benin, and Ghana, resulting in a movement of people to Christ.

Five key principles were at work at Kpele-Dafo.
- The word of God is more effectively communicated through appropriate cultural relationships.
- The word of God will be best heard and understood when we use appropriate oral strategies.
- The word of God is most effectively proclaimed when worldview issues of the unreached are addressed; stories

and other cultural forms do this more effectively by inviting listeners to identify with the message.
- The word of God changes individuals, cultures, and worldviews.
- The word of God can be passed along by ordinary Christians if they receive it in appropriate oral forms.

In both these cases the use of familiar, accepted forms of communicating helped to make the biblical message less foreign. People could easily participate in the event. The word became readily available to them. They entered into the stories and the stories entered into them.

In many parts of the unreached world, there is open hostility to evangelistic activity. Crusades, mass evangelism and public preaching are not welcome. Bible studies and open witnessing draw negative responses. In these situations storying can be more fully appreciated. Storying is not confrontational. It is not preaching. It is not overt teaching. It is merely conveying the stories of God's Word, dialoguing about them and leaving the results to God! Most of the time the hearers do not even realize that their values are changing until they can no longer deny the truth. His word says that it will not return void or empty. So, the power of His word, combined with the power of the Holy Spirit, does amazing things! These stories can go where the printed Bible sometimes cannot go. They can cross borders, enter jail cells, even go into the heart of Muslim, Hindu, animist or socialist homes! They can penetrate the heart of the one listening and change that person's life for eternity.

Making Disciples Of Oral Learners

3

oral
communicators
and
oral
cultures ▶

Oral Communicators
and Oral Cultures

▼

DEVELOPING proficiency in using oral strategies involves several tasks. Literates who want to communicate effectively in oral cultures need to learn about the issue of orality. Walter Ong's book, *Orality and Literacy* (1982) is a respected academic work on the topic. He offers lengthy, technical discussions of the nature of orality and the impact that the development of writing, then typography, had on oral communication and oral cultures. His approach is largely historical.

Another approach to understanding the extent and influence of orality is to consider it in relationship to literacy skills. The reality of low literacy skills even in developed countries has become apparent from a series of surveys, beginning with the National Adult Literacy Survey (NALS) administered by the U. S. Department of Education in the early 1990s.[9] Researchers found that 48 to 51% of adults in the United States scored at the two lowest levels (out of five levels) of measurable proficiency at a range of literacy skills. While results of the NALS study showed that only 4 to 6% of U. S. adults were totally illiterate, 46 to 53%

---

9   Irwin S. Kirsch, Ann Jungeblut, Lynn Jenkins and Andrew Kolstad. *A First Look at the Findings of the National Adult Literacy Survey*, 3d ed. (Washington: U. S. Department of Education, Office of Educational Research and Improvement, 2002).

were identified as unable to function adequately in a highly literate society or process lengthy written information adequately.

It was reported that while many adults at Level 1 (21-23%) could perform tasks involving simple texts and documents, all adults scoring at that level displayed difficulty using certain reading, writing and computational skills considered necessary for functioning in everyday life. Those at Level 2 could perform simple analysis, but were unable to integrate information from longer texts or documents or carry out mathematical skills when necessary information was contained in the directions. (Interestingly enough, a majority of those at Level 1 and almost all of those at Level 2 described themselves as being able to read English "well" or "very well"!).

When the International Adult Literacy Survey (IALS) tested adults in twenty-two countries from 1994-98, similar results emerged in Australia, Canada, Germany, Ireland, the U. K. and elsewhere among developed nations.[10] Although the various governments previously had claimed national literacy rates of 90% or more, the surveys revealed that many people actually had a quite limited range of literacy skills. Such people live day to day largely by oral means even if they are able to read simple, brief materials.

The Bible is certainly not simple, brief material. If half of the population in developed nations, with longstanding literate traditions, is unable to integrate information from a text like the Bible, what is the situation of those in oral cultures with no such tradition, when it comes to gaining spiritual truth?

The survey results from NALS and IALS suggest that there is not a simple, black-and-white dichotomy between "literates" and "illiterates." Other studies similarly give more revealing definitions of literacy that characterize it in terms of the different ways people function with literacy in society. One UNESCO

---

10   See http://www.nifl.gov/nifl/facts/IALS.html. See also Albert Tuijnman, *Benchmarking Adult Literacy in America: An International Comparative Study* (Washington, DC: U. S. Department of Education, 2000); also available at http://www.nald.ca/fulltext/Benchmrk/2.htm. This testing has now been conducted in approximately 30 countries, with similar results.

document, for example, says:

> A person is functionally literate who can engage in all those activities in which literacy is required for effective function of his or her group and community and also for enabling him or her to continue to use reading, writing and calculation for his or her own and the community's development.[11]

It is helpful for literate cross-cultural Christian workers to be aware of different degrees of literacy if they are to communicate with people in appropriate ways. These degrees of literacy reflect a continuum. One categorization of salient points along this continuum is that of James B. Slack, which describes five levels of literacy to be considered in presenting the gospel:

- "Illiterates" cannot read or write. They have never "seen" a word. In fact, the word for illiteracy in the Indonesia language is *buta huruf*, meaning "blind to letters." For oral communicators, words do not exist as letters, but as sounds related to images of events and to situations that they are seeing or experiencing.

- "Functional illiterates" have been to school but do not continue to read and write regularly after dropping out of school. Within two years, even those who have gone to school for eight years often can read only simple sentences and can no longer receive, recall or reproduce concepts, ideas, precepts, and principles through literate means. They prefer to get their information orally. Their *functional* level of illiteracy (as opposed to published data) determines how they learn, how they develop their values and beliefs, and how they pass along their culture, including their religious beliefs and practices.

- "Semi-literates" function in a gray transitional area between oral communication and literacy. Even though these individuals have normally gone to school up to 10 years and are classified in every country of the world as literates,

---

11   http://www.uis.unesco.org/ev.php?ID=5014_201&ID2=DO_TOPIC

they learn primarily by means of narrative presentations.

• "Literate" learners understand and handle information such as ideas, precepts, concepts, and principles by literate means. They tend to rely on printed material as an aid to recall.

• "Highly literate" learners usually have attended college and are often professionals in the liberal arts fields. They are thoroughly print-culture individuals.[12]

Trying to reach the first three categories using customary means presents two major problems: Almost all missionaries and other Christian workers are literate or highly literate, and they communicate primarily by literate means. So they use the method they have mastered to try to communicate with oral learners who do not "hear" them. They think that if they can just simplify their outlines and exposition oral learners can grasp what they are saying. When missionaries try to reach illiterates, they believe that one of their primary tasks is to train a corps of literate nationals (who then face the same problems communicating). For these reasons it is essential that literate church leaders seek to understand orality as the first step in ministering effectively in oral cultures.

Although UNESCO reported in 2003 that almost 80% of adults worldwide can read, that statement is open to challenge.

---

12   James B. Slack, "Chronological Bible Storying" unpublished document available at http:///www.chronologicalbiblestorying.com/manuals.

It depends on literacy statistics provided by each member nation of the United Nations. Furthermore, it allows every country's government to decide for itself how to determine who is literate. Malaysia, for instance, counts anyone age 10 or over who has ever enrolled in school as being literate. Other countries simply ask people if they are literate; many people say that they are, even though their reading skills may be too limited to handle text from the Bible. Many people who can write their name and read a simple sentence qualify as literate for census purposes, but they cannot read unfamiliar or lengthy materials with understanding. Their values are not changed by what they read.

In assessing the orality of a people group, it is important to keep in mind that literacy rates often vary greatly from one group to another within a single nation. Minority language groups, many of whom are unreached peoples, are less likely to be literate. Many of them have little interest in becoming literate. Those who intend to work with unreached people groups would be wise to be skeptical of governmental literacy statistics when it comes to functional literacy.

Missions groups such as the International Mission Board (Southern Baptist Convention), Scriptures In Use and others have developed materials on understanding orality and oral cultures. A selection of these is available at www.chronologicalbiblestorying.com. The annotated bibliography included with this document also suggests a wide array of resources for learning more about orality.

After developing a basic understanding of orality, literate missionaries and ministers then need to learn effective oral communication styles which are culturally relevant. In general, there is a cluster of features that oral learners have in common in processing information. They most readily process information that is concrete and sequential, and which is presented in a highly relational context. Other aspects of an effective communication style for a particular oral culture may be discovered by careful observation and participation in the life of the community.

Using culturally appropriate oral forms improves the impact of the message. Oral learners "enter" the story and as they absorb sensory data they live the story in the present tense—seeing, hearing, tasting, smelling and feeling what the persons in the story are experiencing. They hang reality on these sensory experiences. This happened when "Fatima," an immigrant who had never been to school, attended a class to learn French.[13] As a part of the French class, she heard the story of Abraham, Sarah, and Hagar. At the end of the story Fatima said, "That's a true story."

The teacher asked, "What do you mean?"

Fatima replied, "God made Abraham a promise and Abraham didn't have the faith to wait for God. He acted on his own. And look at all the trouble that came to that family. It happens all the time. People don't have the faith to wait for God. They act on their own and they get into trouble just like Abraham did. It's a true story."

Fatima vicariously lived the story. Without prompting from the teacher, she melded the story's experiences with her experiences. The right cultural form enabled the truth to flow unimpeded into her life.

Having identified the communication forms that the culture uses, it is then crucial that ministries use the existing oral communication forms that the culture already uses (i.e.: story, music, drama, poetry, dance, proverbs, etc.) There are many examples of the impact of Bible stories when time and freedom of expression are both given in order to develop a culturally sensitive storying strategy.

One such example of the effectiveness and reproducibility of using music in orality and storying strategies comes from southeastern Africa:

> The ladies gathered on the lawn for their weekly sewing session. They were in a mountain village about forty kilometres from the shores of Lake Malawi. Usually, as the ladies sewed, they sang. I was visiting the house

---

13   This account is from Annette Hall. When a name is introduced within quote marks, this is an indication that this is a pseudonym. In this and some other subsequent instances, names of local workers and in some cases the people group names in the stories and case studies of this paper are not actual names. The names are changed in order to protect the security of these workers. The events told in the stories and case studies are actual events recounted or confirmed by the participants in the 2004 Lausanne Forum Issue Group on "Making Disciples of Oral Learners."

next door as the ladies began to sing. Because I like music, I enjoyed listening to their singing as I talked with my friends. After a while I heard a tune that was vaguely familiar, but I couldn't place it. I listened harder, concentrating on the music rather than my hosts. Then it hit me! The words and tune I was hearing were the same ones I had heard at a Yao music workshop two weeks before and forty kilometres away! In one day, the group developed fourteen Scripture songs focused on essential stories of God's word. In two weeks the song had travelled across the lake and up the mountain to a village forty kilometres away from where the workshop was held! In their own language they were singing:

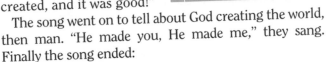

"In the beginning God created, and it was good!
It was good!
In the beginning God created, and it was good!
It was good!
It was good!
It was good!
It was good!
It was good!
In the beginning God created, and it was good!"

The song went on to tell about God creating the world, then man. "He made you, He made me," they sang. Finally the song ended:

"It was good!
It was good!
It was good!
It was good!
All that he had made—yes, it was good!" [14]

An example of how members of an oral culture naturally relate to oral forms of Scripture as their own comes from an experience

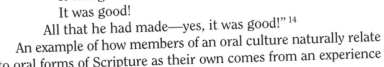

---

14   This account is from Steve Evans.

of Herbert Klem, doing an academic research project involving various test groups:

> One evening I came to a study which was crowded out with visitors. I could tell many of the visitors were Muslim elders from the very community where I was told so often that people felt too old to become Christians. I did not want all those visitors spoiling the structure of my test group, so I politely asked the visitors to leave these Christian test lessons. The wise old elder had a twinkle in his eye as he gently and politely suggested that they were having a wonderful time hearing God speak to them, and that perhaps I should be the one to leave. I did not know what to do. I was thrilled to have a Muslim man in a Bible study, and he was an elder leader, but I did not want to spoil the structure of my test. When I asked him politely to leave a second time, he grinned and challenged me to a true test of ownership of the singing Bible tapes. The one who could sing the least of the tape from memory would leave, and the one who could sing the most could stay. That was the indigenous method of proving cultural ownership.
>
> Because of the tonal intricacies of singing oral art in that language, he knew he had me beat cold — no contest! The group cheered and proclaimed him the owner of the tape. He boasted that only a wise Yoruba man could compose and sing this kind of poetry; insiders loved it and outsiders could admire from a small distance.
>
> The elder had been warmly attracted to the text because it had been identified with his culture, employing art forms that marked it as his cultural property, even though it was played on a tape recorder supplied by a meddling foreigner. He was pleased with the form of the message, but he was also bonding with God's Word from the book of Hebrews. He was no longer telling me this was "foreign religion" but was

defending his right to hear the Scripture. Best of all, the whole group loved the entire event.[15]

In addition to the choice of communication form, the choice of what language to use is crucial. The most effective ministry strategies among oral cultures occur when the communication is done in the heart language, the mother tongue. It is often easy to overlook the fact that people speaking over 4,000 different languages are still awaiting God's word in their heart language. Many of these groups have a long history of being a minority people in their own country. When the Bible has come to them in the past, it has often been in a printed form that they cannot read or in a language which does not speak to their heart. In fact, it might be in the language of the very people who they feel have oppressed them for many years.

However, when they hear the stories from God's word in their own language, they are often amazed and have an immediate heart response and cultural identification with that message. They may respond that indeed God has remembered them and He is for them! When they hear the message in their heart language, the words speak to them in an indescribable way. Because it is their own language, it captivates them and they want to hear more.

Stories heard in the mother tongue are easily memorized and retold to others. Oral learners can often recite large portions of scripture when they hear these passages in their mother tongue and packaged in the stories that they can easily learn and reproduce.

Effective ministries among oral cultures should be worldview sensitive in order to build bridges of understanding and confront barriers to the gospel message. Because stories possess the power to actually change how people think, feel, and behave, and to change the way they see the world, it is important to have a sequential, step-by-step process that leads them to a new, biblical worldview. What is effective in such situations is the oral communication of a set of chronological Bible stories that involve points of similarity between a culture's worldview and a biblical worldview. This

---

15   Herbert Klem, "Dependence on Literacy Strategy: Taking a Hard Second Look," *International Journal of Frontier Missions* 12:2 (April-June, 1995) 63-64.

incorporates "bridges" from its worldview to the biblical story. It simultaneously confronts "barriers" to the gospel, those elements of the worldview that hinder understanding and acceptance. Over time, confronting worldview barriers with stories of the Bible can lead them to accept a more compelling story than the stories associated with their own worldview.

An example of this account comes from the Asheninka people group in Peru:

> Alejandro, the leader, is doing great in chronological Bible storying and the people understand. He told the story of Jesus calming the waters during the storm and Cladis softly told me that she used to believe that the Owner of the Winds could be stopped by placing your axe in the ground with the blade cutting the wind, but now she knows it is God that created the winds and He is God. Also, she told me that she is not scared of the rainbows anymore because they do not kill you when you walk under them. God created the rainbow to make a promise with us. Alejandro himself came to the understanding that he can baptize the people and the people understand that they can be baptized after simply believing. So, Alejandro baptized twelve believers last week. It was a week of fiestas. Trip after trip Alejandro tells the stories, *then*, it hits them. It is such an awesome thing to be part of.[16]

Choosing stories that address worldview bridges and barriers of a specific people group or segment of society improves the likelihood that their worldview will be brought into conformity with the biblical pattern, the kingdom of God.

Understanding orality and oral cultures gives us the basis for adopting effective oral communications strategies. These understandings enable us to realize the importance of the word being shared in the mother tongue and in ways that enable the people to embrace the message from God.

---

16   This account comes from Pam Ammons, and can be found, along with other examples at: http://www.chronologicalbiblestorying.com/news/newsletters_index.htm.

4
disciples
to the core

Disciples to the Core

SYNCRETISM is "the mixing of Christian assumptions with those worldview assumptions that are incompatible with Christianity so that the result is not biblical Christianity."[17] Syncretism weakens the church, warps non-Christians' understanding of Christianity and withholds from God the full devotion and complete obedience that is rightly due to Him. So the spiritual health and vibrancy of Christian churches depends on developing a faith that is as free from syncretism as possible, a faith that is both biblical and culturally relevant. Several key elements can contribute to discipling oral learners with a minimal amount of syncretism.

The first key element in avoiding syncretism is communicating with people in their mother tongue — the language in which they learned their religion, values and cultural identity. They house their innermost thoughts in their mother tongue, so it is the language through which their worldview is most likely to change. They can explain their new faith more readily to others in their people group when they use the mother tongue. In using the

---

17   Charles Kraft, "Culture, Worldview and Contextualization," in *Perspectives on the World Christian Movement*, 3d ed., ed. Ralph D. Winter and Steven C. Hawthorne (Pasadena, CA: William Carey Library, 1999), 390.

mother tongue, one must carefully consider the key biblical terms to use in a language if there is not yet a Bible translation. Concepts like love, grace and sin, or even the basic notion like the name used for God, the Holy Spirit, or Christ need to be carefully identified. Inadequacies in this area readily lead to syncretism.

When pastors are asked why they preach in a national language or trade language instead of the local language of their congregation, they often respond that they did their theological training in the trade language and that the local language is not rich in theological terms. If the pastor does not know how to express theological terms in the local language, you can be sure that his people are not grasping these important concepts. When the pastor does not preach and teach in the local language, he is leaving the important task of choosing the correct term to interpreters who do not have the benefit of the pastor's theological training. The use of interpreters who are not trained in biblical language can result in wrong words being used for important Christian concepts and this can lead to syncretism or even heresy.

The Puinave people of Colombia were "re-discipled" when missionaries uncovered syncretism.[18] Although the Puinave had become culturally "Christian" in the 1950s, they mixed magic with their understanding of Christianity's behavioral norms. Many misunderstandings resulted from using the national language, Spanish, in their Christian activity. When New Tribes Mission workers spent seven years learning the Puinave language in the 1970s, they were surprised at the syncretistic beliefs held. At first, they tried teaching the Bible using traditional teaching methods. The Puinave nodded their agreement, but missed many of the key points.

It was only through a chronological presentation of God's word, beginning with the Old Testament and on to the Gospels, story by story, that they were able to vividly portray the holy nature and character of God, the sinful condition of man, the grip that Satan has on this world and the redeeming solution to man's predicament found in Jesus Christ. Reflecting on this

---

18   New Tribes Mission, *Now We See Clearly*, video, 1998.

redemptive panorama of God's provision, the village elder held up his thumb near to his forefinger and observed: "I came just this close from going to hell..."

Consider the example of Jesus. He taught using the common heart language of the people, rather than the trade language. Jesus spoke in the format that the common people understood such as stories, parables and proverbs. The people who heard were able to understand and apply them, bringing about transformed lives. By communicating in the heart language and using the methods that are common in the culture, we can minimize the danger of syncretism and heresy.

A second key element in reducing syncretism is to develop discipling resources that are worldview specific. Generic discipleship materials are insufficient. Certainly there are biblical essentials that every new Christian needs to know, such as prayer, worship, witness, fellowship and ministry. These practices, however, should fit the local culture under the leadership of the Holy Spirit rather than the practices of the host culture of the missionary. Kraft points out that syncretism occurs when the evangelizers impose their cultural values on the new Christians and fail to separate the evangelizers' own culture adequately from the biblical message.[19] If a certain set of discipleship materials worked well with a people group or segment of society, it is because the materials were meaningful to that worldview. The fact that they served so well among one people should serve as a caution that they will not likely meet needs as effectively in a different cultural setting.

The best discipling resource among oral communicators is not a printed booklet but an obedient Christian. Oral communicators learn by observing. Discipleship involves the disciple spending time with the more mature believer learning by following his or her example. The teaching is conducted more by watching and doing rather than just learning facts. Discipling oral learners would best follow the biblical models such as Elijah, Jesus, and Paul. For example, Paul tells the

---

19   Charles Kraft, "Culture, Worldview and Contextualization," 390.

Philippian believers, *"Whatever you have learned or received or heard from me, or seen in me–put it into practice"* (Phil. 4:9 NIV). The goal would be that the disciple would immediately become a discipler. As Paul told Timothy, *". . . the things you have heard me say in the presence of many witnesses entrust to reliable men who will also be qualified to teach others"* (2 Tim. 2:2 NIV).

A third key element in discipling oral learners in order to limit syncretism is to recognize the importance of stories in transforming a person's worldview. N. T. Wright says that stories constitute the core of every culture's worldview. (See the diagram below.) A culture houses its central convictions in its fundamental narrative, whether its narrative is implicit or explicit. The ancient mythologies that we find in cultures around the world are explicit examples of this. Those stories answer four fundamental worldview questions: Who am I? Where am I? What has gone wrong? What can be done about it? Every culture uses stories to tell us what it means to be human, what kind of world we live in, why there is suffering and pain, and what, if anything, we can do to deal with that suffering and pain. Christianity has its own distinctive answers to those worldview questions. In order to influence the worldviews of disciples, we need to tell biblical stories that offer alternative answers to the fundamental worldview questions. The Bible answers these questions with special vividness and power in the opening chapters of Genesis.[20] That is one reason it is so important to include Old Testament stories in discipling. Furthermore, when we tell biblical stories chronologically, we

---

20   What God has done to deal with the problem of sin is revealed much more fully in the Gospels and Epistles, of course, but there are references to God's redemptive plan in the early stories in Genesis.

are offering a powerful alternative worldview from the very beginning of our presentation. Biblical stories, and the view of the world embedded in them, can replace or refine the cultural stories and the worldview embedded in them.

Wright argues that this is why Jesus so often told stories, particularly parables. Jesus intended them to challenge the existing Jewish worldview and to provide an alternative picture of reality that Jesus called "the kingdom of God" or "kingdom of heaven." Wright says, "Stories are, actually, peculiarly good at modifying or subverting other stories and their worldviews. Where head-on attack would certainly fail, the parable hides the wisdom of the serpent behind the innocence of the dove, gaining entrance and favour which can then be used to change assumptions which the hearer would otherwise keep hidden away for safety."[21]

There are four areas that affect people...

The Transforming Power Of Stories!

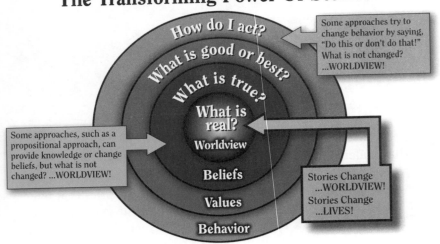

How do I act?

What is good or best?

What is true?

What is real?

Worldview

Beliefs

Values

Behavior

Some approaches try to change behavior by saying, "Do this or don't do that!" What is not changed? ...WORLDVIEW!

Some approaches, such as a propositional approach, can provide knowledge or change beliefs, but what is not changed? ...WORLDVIEW!

Stories Change ...WORLDVIEW! Stories Change ...LIVES!

Wright says stories come into conflict with each other because worldviews and the stories which characterize them

21   N. T. Wright, *The New Testament and the People of God*, (Minneapolis: Fortress Press, 1992), 40.

represent the realities of one's life. People are threatened by the intrusion of an opposing worldview or story because it challenges their understanding of reality. Wright says *"The only way of handling the clash between two stories is to tell yet another story explaining how the evidence for the challenging story is in fact deceptive."*[22]

If stories anchor people's existing perspective on the world, then the best thing Christians can do in order to displace that perspective is to tell better stories, and we have them! Our stories must provide biblical answers to the essential questions of life.[23] The more biblical stories people know and can fit into a single comprehensive story of God's saving work, the more completely they are able to embrace a biblical worldview. By changing their fundamental view of the world, we hope to influence a wide array of beliefs and practices which grow out of that fundamental core.

Wright argues that stories lie at the core of a worldview; formal belief statements, including propositional and theological statements, grow out of those stories. Thus discipleship that offers only propositional teaching does not reach to the centre of the worldview. If we give only propositional teaching and do not present biblical *stories* to challenge existing worldview *stories*, we run the risk of syncretism. The cultural stories will continue to comprise the heart of the worldview and discipleship will deal only with the dimensions of the person's life represented in the outer circles in the diagram. Because propositional beliefs are generated by and reflected in the core stories, those cultural stories will continually be challenging the Christian propositional content. We wind up with the tragedy of professing Christians who assent to biblical propositions, but whose essential worldview and value system is deeply tied to worldview stories that have gone unchallenged. That mix of contradictory religious beliefs and practices is the essence of syncretism. It constitutes a failure in discipling.

A careful study of an unreached people group's worldview will reveal common ground, bridges between their worldview and

---

22   Wright, 42.
23   Wright, 38-40.

the Bible. On these matters the discipler may simply *reinforce* existing beliefs and practices. Worldview study also will disclose matters on which the people group's worldview is contrary to the biblical ideal; these contrary matters are barriers.[24] In those instances, the discipler guides converts to *replace* the existing belief or practice with the biblical one. In addition, the study may reveal issues in which the existing practices and beliefs can be *revised* into the way of Christ. This approach to discipling aims to minimize the syncretism that comes when people just adopt Christian rituals or practices, but keep intact the mythology that underlies the traditional religion. When their core stories are not challenged and replaced, the traditional mythology will continue and may over time infuse the Christian practices with meanings from the traditional religion.

A fourth key element in order to avoid syncretism is to provide a recorded "oral Bible" for each people group in their language. This is a recorded set of stories, biblically accurate and told in the worldview context. At this point the "oral Bible" may be the only scriptural resource available to oral learners. At some future time when written Bible translation is completed, then it could be recorded to provide a standard point of reference.

In an "oral Bible," the stories are communicated in natural, live situations by mother tongue "storyers" from the people group, using the mannerisms and storytelling techniques which are appropriate to that people group. The Bible stories are checked to ensure biblical accuracy before recording takes place. By utilizing this system that checks the stories as they are told, it will ensure that this recorded "oral Bible" is a plumb line for oral methods such as stories, song, etc.

By telling Bible stories in a straightforward way, we give new converts an opportunity to engage biblical truth directly and discover its message for themselves. This approach is significantly different from the approach that has people read numerous individual verses sequenced according to the

---

24   Detailed examples and training resources on how to conduct a worldview study can be found on the website www.chronologicalbiblestorying.com

curriculum writer's sense of importance and logic and largely divorced from their biblical context. Telling a biblical story in an interesting and accurate way is a simple but powerful manner of freeing disciples to process Scripture. They can do it with a minimum of filtering and interpretive baggage coming from the discipler's culture and experience of Christianity. This is especially true when we tell the stories in chronological order, thus putting them in a biblical context.

The practice of keeping the story *pure* (separate from our own comments and interpretive remarks) protects the oral learners from the syncretism that might come from embracing a polished system of ethics, theology or pastoral philosophy that has a significant dose of European, North American, Korean, Brazilian or Chinese cultural baggage. Instead they synthesize a biblical theology from the stories and can apply it in all kinds of practical situations with courage.

In summary, those of us who seek to make disciples of oral learners will want them to understand biblical truth and live obedient lives as free from syncretism as possible. We can increase the likelihood of that happening when we disciple in the mother tongue, use worldview-specific approaches instead of generic ones, utilize biblical stories extensively and work with mother-tongue speakers to produce an "oral Bible" that provides a reliable repository of biblical truth.

5

reproducibility,
reproducibility,
reproducibility

Reproducibility, Reproducibility, Reproducibility

MANY people accept the idea that an oral approach like chronological Bible storying may be appropriate to initial evangelism, but they wonder whether a storying approach is viable for a sustained, indigenous-led church planting movement. Is it adequate for sustained discipleship among second, third and successive generations and for leadership development in the church? Those working in storying in face-to-face, relational societies assert that not only is it a viable approach to meet these needs—it is the preferred approach to ensure reproducibility and thus sustainability in an emerging, indigenous-led church.

For a spiritual movement to be engaged, we must consciously choose strategies that oral learners can easily reproduce. We must constantly evaluate whether we are modeling the kind of disciples we want the learners to become. This is the most powerful form of discipling. Oral communicators learn best when they pattern themselves after those who led them to Christ. From our first contact with non-Christians, we are modeling how a Christian relates to non-Christians and seeks to introduce them to Jesus Christ. Thus even our evangelism is in this sense a part of discipling.

The first and most basic aspect of ensuring reproducibility

in a storying approach is crafting and telling stories in a way that the hearers are able to readily learn and tell themselves and thus effect a reproducing evangelism. This is why we place great importance on the live, natural telling of stories by mother tongue storyers in the common situations where people communicate with one another. When the gospel is communicated to an oral learner in a way that shows dependence on a written or recorded presentation, it inhibits this reproducibility.

A storyer from Senegal reported:

> Recently one of the oral learners told all of us the story of Cain and Abel. She was very accurate, animated, and told all of it from memory. She also led the discussion time with questions. The truly amazing part is that she had missed the previous week's lesson and had learned the story at midweek prayer meeting from another woman who had been present for the training. This oral learner had learned the story from one who had herself just learned the story and had learned to tell it. Some of their children who attend the study with them have prayed: 'Thank You that our mother is now able to teach us the Bible.' [25]

A similar case is reported among the Santal people of South Asia.[26] Village literacy among this people group was found to be 0.08%. The Santal people have no written history and do not rely on written documents for evidence or for credibility. They rely on what the elders have decided or what the elders say. A Christian outreach effort went to a Santal village and met Marandi, a man who had never been to school. They presented the gospel using oral methods, including stories, visual aids, dramas, songs, dances, and testimonies. Marandi trusted Christ and shared his testimony with his family, who also believed and were baptized. He then went to other relatives and shared his new faith with them, using many of the same oral methods. They also believed and were baptized.

---

25   From http://www.chronologicalbiblestorying.com/news/newsletters, Oct 2001, Vol. 8, No 4.

26   This account is provided by S. D. Ponraj and Sheila Ponraj

He then formed a team of believers, all oral communicators, who went to neighbouring villages using the same combination of stories, dramas, songs, etc. People in those villages accepted Christ, too. Those new believers formed their own teams and they went to yet other villages, still using the same basic strategies that had been introduced in the beginning. Many Santal people believed and they then formed their own outreach teams. The movement continues today among the Santal people.

Other stories and case studies attest that discipling, church planting and developing leaders are also effectively done by a storying approach. First consider a story that shows effective discipling within an oral, storying approach.

In a dusty village in southwestern Nigeria, "Timothy" serves faithfully as pastor of a young church consisting of Yoruba farmers and their families.[27] Three years into his pastorate, Timothy had the opportunity to attend a short course for pastors on chronological Bible storying. There he learned the ancient way of teaching that was new to him. He was encouraged to tell Bible stories in an accurate and interesting way and then lead the group to retell the story, discuss its meaning, and relate the truths to their lives. Upon arriving home, Timothy decided that on the following Sunday he would try out what he had learned.

Because the conference leader had recommended telling Bible stories in chronological sequence, Timothy decided to begin with the story of the creation of spirit beings. He drew on several biblical passages to formulate this particular story as had been illustrated in the short course. After asking them about their creation stories and getting no response, Timothy told the Yoruba creation story. He used that as a bridge to the biblical narration of the story of the creation of angelic beings. He presented it as a story—without explaining it or exhorting the group. Afterward, he asked for someone to retell the biblical story and someone did. Then he asked them questions and led in a dialogue that helped them understand and apply the story.

"It was thrilling to me that someone was able to tell the story

---

27   This account is provided by Grant Lovejoy.

and others made corrections," he later reported. "The people were very eager to hear more of the stories. When they began to ask questions that were beyond the story, I did not answer [their questions] but simply told them, 'as I tell more stories, you will discover that yourself.'"

Timothy explained, "I have come to understand that they are more open to ask questions with this method, unlike when I was using the [denominational] Sunday School book. Even the children were answering questions. So it is good for the children too. I have decided to train someone by sharing the story on Saturday with the person so that he or she can share with the children on Sunday.

"I also discovered as I asked them questions and listened to their questions that they were still holding on to their previous teachings of worshipping angels," Timothy explained. "To them the angels are from heaven and can reach God better, so we can pass through them to God. This session has further taught me that they have not understood my topical sermons. It now gives me the opportunity to explain to them things on this issue which I do not normally preach on."

Timothy used the same approach the next Sunday, telling the story of the creation of the heavens and the earth. After this second storying session with them, he commented, "Some of their questions during the session have made me understand that they have not understood many things from the Bible for these three years [that he had been their pastor]."

Timothy discovered several important lessons about making disciples. He realized that to effectively disciple, one must first determine how one's people learn. Although Timothy had pastored his people for three years, he had not been aware that his preaching style needed to match the people's learning style. They lived in a relational culture with a strong oral tradition.

They passed on their history in stories and proverbs. Timothy became conscious of the fact that he was a literate pastor trained in literate teaching methods. The methods he had been taught to use worked well among people highly educated in western schools, but they didn't work well in his situation. He decided to return to his cultural roots as well as model his preaching and teaching after the greatest teacher–Jesus.

Before Timothy changed his teaching methods, he had been frustrated by his people's lack of response. He thought the problem was theirs, that perhaps they were not very intelligent. When Timothy changed his methods the people responded and he discerned that he had been the problem because he had not been communicating effectively. He said, "I have learned to be patient with learners and not to condemn them rashly when they give some 'stupid' answers that are not relevant to what we are discussing. This has encouraged most that didn't use to respond to questions to do so now."

An oral, storying approach can likewise be effective for church planting. A recent church planting movement took place in South Asia among a highly oral people.[28] The oral peoples consisted of various scheduled castes, some of whom were animists while others were of Hindu religious background. From 1997-2003 an agricultural project combined with a chronological Bible storying approach led to approximately two thousand new church starts. An expatriate strategy coordinator worked with two media specialists—one a national and one an expatriate—to develop the biblical stories and the communications strategies. The stories were chosen and crafted with biblical accuracy to engage the people at their worldview values and beliefs level. The stories that were told in the villages were the same stories they heard through the FEBA radio broadcasts. The media specialist and FEBA provided taped recordings that served to improve the hearers' memory of the stories. The local Christian farmers, who were trained in implementing vital agricultural and health technologies, mentored other farmers even on large plantations.

---

28   This account is provided by James B. Slack.

In using those technologies, they told the Bible stories in sequence in the evenings after the agriculture sessions. Those who demonstrated further interest in the Bible stories they heard were invited into Bible story listening groups focused on the radio broadcasts. In the groups they would hear the stories told again but in those groups they were organized to discuss the stories as they heard them. Later the stories were also told face to face by those who became interested in the stories and who embraced Jesus Christ as Lord and Saviour. Again, the stories were circulated on audiocassette. It is important to understand that the stories heard on the radio, the stories told in the fields and villages, and the stories heard on the cassettes were the same stories.

Thousands of believers have come from this wedding of agricultural, health and storytelling technologies. As this church planting movement continues to escalate through these partner methods, the locals are now addressing aberrant doctrinal beliefs through stories. An independent evaluation of this situation revealed a situation where the lay pastors discipled and trained by oral methods maintained essentially correct doctrine, compared to more literate pastors in the same people group, trained by literate means, who exhibited syncretized doctrinal positions. This group dates its origin to a preacher who came in the 1760s. They had about 250 churches when the multiplication of churches began through the storying approaches. Since they began storying, they have gone from a mathematical average of approximately one new church a year to approximately one new church a day.

Another example of church planting using similar storying strategies comes from Romania.[29] Expatriate church planting strategists with the Deaf were involved in a storying approach with associates in planting five Deaf churches. Those among the Romanian Deaf community who became believers through a storying approach in those five church plants went on to plant twenty more Deaf churches. They used the telling of their own testimonies in their heart language, Romanian Sign Language,

---

29   This account is provided by Mark Sauter and Vesta Sauter

47

coupled with chronological Bible storying.

Deaf communities have many of the same features that characterize oral communicators. In fact, a more comprehensive way of looking at what are called "orality" features is not that they are crucially or exclusively associated with what is spoken

by mouth. They are, instead a correlation of ways of processing that are common to face-to-face, highly relational societies. The correlation of ways of processing and communicating involve concrete (rather than abstract) notions; sequential (rather than random) expression of events; and relational (as opposed to individualist) contexts. Both oral cultures and Deaf communities exhibit these characteristics because they are face-to-face, highly relational cultures. Throughout the world, Deaf communities are being reached by chronological Bible storying methods. So there is reason to include them in this discussion. (It is in some sense inaccurate to call the Deaf "oral communicators." Furthermore, they dislike the terms "oral," "orality" and "oralism" because they associate the terms with nineteenth and twentieth century efforts to force the Deaf to give up sign language and learn to speak.)

An account of oral, storying strategies that were effective in leadership development comes from North Africa.[30] There 17 young men (many of whom could barely read and write and some not at all) underwent a two-year leader training program using chronological Bible storying. At the end of two years, students mastered approximately 135 biblical stories in their correct

---

30   This account is provided by Grant Lovejoy.

chronological order, spanning from Genesis to Revelation. They were able to tell the stories, sing from one to five songs for each story, and enact dramas about each of the stories. A seminary professor gave them a six-hour oral exam. They demonstrated the ability to answer questions about both the facts and theology of the stories and showed an excellent grasp of the gospel message, the nature of God, and their new life in Christ. The students quickly and skillfully referred to the stories to answer a variety of theological questions. Given a theological theme, they could accurately name multiple biblical stories in which that theme occurs. If asked, they could tell each story and elaborate on how it addressed the theme.

The professor concluded that "the training process has successfully achieved its goals of enabling students to tell a large number of biblical stories accurately, to have a good understanding of those stories and the theology that they convey and to have an eagerness to share the Christian message. The community received the stories and story-songs enthusiastically and have made them part of the culture and church life alike."

"Various students acknowledged that they entered knowing little of the Old Testament, did not understand the relationship between God and Jesus, did not know the characteristics of God, did not know that God created the angelic beings, had not heard of being born again and did not know that Christians should not seek help from local deities. Upon entering the program these students were unable to communicate the Christian faith to other people, but by the time the training was over, they had dramatically improved their understanding of all of these matters and many more," he said. The songs and stories became so popular that when the students returned to their villages, the local people eagerly gathered to learn the new songs and stories, and frequently sang the Scripture songs and told the stories late into the night, sometimes even until dawn.

The stories and case studies above illustrate various aspects of reproducibility among relational-narrative communicators, both among oral communicators and the Deaf. One important aspect of this involves them telling the story of their own experience of coming to faith in Christ. Those from face-to-face societies readily testify to their personal, daily relationship with Christ. Testimony times in worship services in Western services are limited or non-existent. However, among oral communicators, testimony and prayer times may take up most of the service. When friends and neighbours hear these testimonies and see the change in new converts' lives, they often want to follow the "Jesus road." After they have come to Christ through a process of biblical revelation through stories, the discipler helps them learn an abridged story of the gospel message to use immediately. Disciplers then encourage them to give others the opportunity to hear the biblical stories they heard, in order to consolidate their faith and give these new believers a biblical foundation. Multiple church planting and discipleship efforts from the U. S. to China now incorporate a "my story, your story, God's story, others' stories approach."

Discipling oral communicators involves identifying what the new believers need to know and do and then communicating these truths using appropriate methods. These methods include modeling, telling a Bible story that communicates a truth, discussing it, perhaps memorizing a Scripture related to the matter and applying the truth together or individually. Their discipleship is shaped by the modeling of another believer and on-the-job training. This is most effective when the modeling is done by an in-culture or close-culture believer. Discipleship is not just what one does but who one is—a new creature in Christ. Then we must help them understand that discipleship is primarily a matter of obedience to everything Jesus commanded and revealed in Scripture.

Discipling involves having the disciple do all of the preceding plus being held accountable to report back. This model of discipleship emphasizes accountability for application in two crucial dimensions: living it and sharing it with others. Oral learners, like all true followers of Jesus, need to practice what Scripture teaches and to pass along to others what they are learning.

Oral communicators are more dependent on relationships in communication than literate learners are. For that reason oral communicators tend to place a higher value on those relationships. They believe persons more than abstract truths. So the spiritual life and modeling of the messenger is crucial. Making disciples of oral communicators requires maintaining a loving relationship with the ones being discipled. Disciplers help oral communicators acquire biblical truth through appropriate oral means and guide them to obey it. Disciplers also teach them to win and disciple others who will in turn disciple others. The new converts join existing churches or form new churches, according to the situation.

Discipling oral communicators should lead directly to church planting as new converts come together in covenant communities of believers to carry out the functions of the church. In many instances, these will be house churches that develop along lines of kinship and friendship. Disciples grow best when, from the beginning of their Christian experience, they take responsibility for evangelizing, nurturing new converts, establishing new works and overseeing the development of their own converts.

Providing orally based leader training for oral learners and equipping them to continue it within their people group is one of the great challenges facing the Church. Those involved in rapidly growing church planting movements must disciple and equip leaders for the new churches as leaders are raised up by the Holy Spirit. If they do not, the expansion of the movement slows or ceases.

A summarization of the storying approach from the CD series, *Following Jesus: Making Disciples of Oral Learners*, specifies a ten-step process toward making disciples of primary oral learners with reproducibility as the important culminating step:

- *Identify* the biblical principle that you want to communicate – simply and clearly.

- *Evaluate* the worldview issues of the chosen people group.
- *Consider* worldview – the bridges, barriers, and gaps.
- *Select* the biblical stories that are needed to communicate the biblical principle.
- *Plan* (craft) the story and plan the dialogue that is going to follow the story, focusing on the task to be accomplished.
- *Communicate* the story in a culturally appropriate way, using narrative, song, dance, object lessons, and other forms.
- *Apply* the principle by facilitating dialogue with the group, helping them to discover the meaning and application of the story to their own lives.
- *Obey* the discovered principle by implementation steps to be taken by the individuals.
- *Accountability* – establish accountability between group members by mutual and reciprocal commitments to implement the biblical principle in the conduct of their personal lives between members of the group, their families and other personal relationships.
- *Reproduce* – encourage the group to reproduce the biblical principle, first by demonstrating the principle in their own "witness of life" then in sharing the principle with others. [31]

Bible storying provides a way of engaging a people group that is not highly technological and can readily involve oral communicators in efforts to reach their own people group with the gospel. Storying is thus a reproducible evangelistic and church planting approach—new believers can readily share the gospel, plant new churches and disciple new believers in the same way that they themselves were reached and discipled.

While a storying strategy seems to be one that is particularly appropriate with unreached people groups, many involved with people groups where there is an established church have found significant benefits to a chronological storying approach in those situations as well. The oral, chronological approach

---

31   *Following Jesus: Making Disciples of Primary Oral Learners,* hosted by Avery T. Willis Jr., Progressive Vision, 2002.

can fill major gaps that literate approaches to evangelism, discipling, church planting and leadership development have, over the decades, missed.

6

when literates

stop reading

When Literates
Stop Reading

RECALL the statement that two-thirds of the world's people can't, won't, or don't read and write. The bulk of this paper has focused on those who can't. This part will focus on those who don't. These are those who choose to learn by oral methods as opposed to literate ones, in spite of their literacy. These people are known as secondary oral learners. James B. Slack defines "secondary oral learners" as "people who have become literate because of their job or schooling, but prefer to be entertained, learn and communicate by oral means." Walter Ong, father of the modern orality movement, says, "I style the orality of a culture totally untouched by writing or print, 'primary orality.' It is 'primary' by contrast with the 'secondary orality' of present-day high-technology culture, in which a new orality is sustained by telephone, radio, television and other electronic devices that depend for their existence and functioning on writing and print."[32]

Earlier in this paper we explored the characteristics of oral learners. It is increasingly evident that many of these same characteristics are as descriptive of secondary oral learners as they are of primary oral learners. As such, the effectiveness of our

---

32   Ong, Walter J. *Orality & Literacy: The Technologizing of the World* (London and New York: Routledge, 1982).

communication is dependent on what we do with this knowledge.

Our purpose is to call missions-minded Christians to explore ways to be more effective in communicating with secondary oral learners—in reaching them for Christ, helping them grow and mobilizing them to involvement in ministry.

Why is it important to do this? A 2004 study reported that "literary reading in America is not only declining rapidly among all groups, but the rate of decline has accelerated, especially among the young." This reflects a "massive shift toward electronic media for entertainment and information."[33] Numerous western societies are seeing similar shifts toward electronic media and the accompanying secondary orality.

Consider the following statistics:

- 58% of the U. S. adult population never read another book after high school.

- 42% of U. S. university graduates never read another book.

- Adults in the U. S. spend four hours per day watching TV, three hours listening to the radio and 14 minutes reading magazines.[34]

- British teenagers' pleasure reading declined by about a third from 1991-1998.[35]

- In Denmark one-third of adults do not do any significant amount of reading.[36]

- More than half the adults in the Netherlands hardly ever

---

33   *Reading at Risk: A Survey of Literary Reading in America,* Research Division Report no. 46 (Washington, DC: National Endowment for the Arts, 2004), vii. The term "literary reading" includes books such as romance novels, so these statistics reflect pleasure reading generally, not just the reading of "literary classics." The survey included 17,000 adults and was administered by the U. S. Census Bureau.
34   The first three items are reported by Dan Poynter and cited in http://newwway.org/news/2004/apr 2.htm.
35   *Young People in 1998,* a report compiled from surveys of 18,221 pupils by the Schools Health Education Unit based at Exeter University. Available at http://www.sheu.org.uk/pubs/yp98.htm.
36   Viggo Sogaard, *Evangelizing Our World: Insights from Global Inquiry* (Pattaya, Thailand: 2004 Forum for World Evangelization, 2004), 11.

read a book. [37]

- Dutch 12 year old school children spend, on average, less than half an hour a week reading in their leisure time.

Apparently, related trends are unfolding elsewhere in the world.

"Reading and writing are clearly dying arts," professor Jim Dator of the University of Hawaii said, "something which fewer in the world are doing." More important, he said, is the fact that reading and writing are something fewer and fewer people need to know how to do. "Most people in the world, even most of the literate people in the world in fact, do not get much of their ideas about the world from reading. They get them from watching television, going to the movies, listening to the radio, and other forms of audio-visual communication." [38]

Ravi Zacharias, a Christian apologist, agrees. "More and more we are knowing less and less about the printed tradition," he said. "The ability for abstract reasoning is diminishing in our time, because [people] come to their conclusions on the basis of images. Their capacity for abstract reasoning is gone." Zacharias concludes that we are now in a time where there is a "humiliation of the word" and an "exaltation of the image." [39]

In their book *Church Next: Quantum Changes in Christian Ministry*, Eddie Gibbs and Ian Coffey also conclude that people

---

37   Both statements about reading in the Netherlands are from Marieke Sanders-ten Holte, "Creating an Optimum Reading Culture in the Low Countries: The Role of Stichting Lezen," a paper presented at the 64th International Federation of Library Associations and Institutions General Conference, Aug.16-21, 1998, Amsterdam, http://www.ifla.org/IV/ifla64/098-80e.htm.

38   Jim Dator, "Families, Communities, and Futures," http://www.soc.hawaii.edu/future/dator/other/FCF.html

39   Ravi Zacharias, "Mind Games in a World of Images," audiotape.

today are more influenced by audio and visual media than print media. "Theirs is a post-literacy culture for which sound and image have largely replaced the printed word," they claim. The two argue that "instancy" and intimacy are the distinguishing features of today's non-print media, and that seeing, not reading, is the basis for believing.[40]

Pritish Nandi, publisher and television news producer in India, recently wrote an article titled "Will Technology Usher in an Era of Illiteracy?" In it he said, "New technology will no longer divide the world into literate and illiterate people but will bring everyone together in a common platform where the ability to read and write will no longer matter. You will have a new world where people will need an entirely different kind of skills set to succeed."[41]

All of these examples are clear indications of a growing global emergence of secondary orality, or post-literacy as some call it. This phenomenon is causing us to think, communicate, process information, and make decisions more and more like oral peoples. The implications of this have ramifications not only on what we do in evangelism, discipleship, leader training and church planting, but also on how we do it! We must make adjustments in the way we communicate the message of the gospel, acknowledging that our goal, responsibility, and desire are to communicate truth in the most effective ways possible.

For many of us, it is becoming more and more evident that issues of secondary orality are reaching the very altars of our churches around the world. Christian researcher George Barna said that technology and the mass media have forever changed the ways in which we process information, saying that "the inability to systematically apply scriptural truth produces a spiritual superficiality or immaturity that is reflected in behaviour." He concludes that we must develop new forums and formats through which people will experience, understand, and serve God.[42]

---

40   Eddie Gibbs and Ian Coffey, *Church Next: Quantum Changes in Christian Ministry* (Leicester, England: Inter-Varsity Press, 2001), 127.
41   *The International Indian*, 9:4, (August 2001), 22.
42   George Barna, *The Second Coming of the Church: A Blue Print for Survival* (Nashville: Word Publishing, 1998).

Tommy Jones, author of *Postmodern Youth Ministry,* urges us to tell stories. "Narrative is becoming the primary means of telling beliefs. Since propositional logic has fallen on hard times, stories carry more weight in carrying truths – "abductive" reasoning. As opposed to deductive or inductive methods, when you tell a story, you 'abduct' listeners from their known worlds into another world."[43]

Rick Durst, academic dean at Golden Gate Seminary in California, agrees. "To be a 'storyteller' is no longer a euphemism for someone with a loose grip on truth," he said. "The storyteller is becoming again the person of wisdom who knows the 'good telling stories' that make and maintain community and meaning." Durst refers to well-known Christian author Leonard Sweet, who sees pastors as "story doctors," who use the "truthing" of biblical stories to heal the dysfunctional stories confining and confounding people's lives, concluding that ministry to the emerging generation will be magnified to the degree that narrative is applied.[44]

How do we get started? First, we need to pray that God will show us how to be more effective. We need to ask for ways to turn what have been barriers into bridges. Second, we need to be observant of what is already proven in how to communicate with literate people who have at least some preference for learning orally. For example, many graduate programs in business administration use case study discussions to teach essential leadership principles. As another example, many of the most effective evangelistic speakers and pastors use stories to illustrate their message points. Dallas Theological Seminary professor Howard Hendricks is quoted as saying that such illustrations are the windows to the soul. As a third example, many who teach the Bible in small groups have discovered that a way to understanding is for the student to see specifically how a Bible truth looks when it is applied. If the leader is able to share his or her own experience (story) with how this works, learning is

---

43 Tommy Jones, *Postmodern Youth Ministry* (Grand Rapids: Zondervan, 2001), 27.
44 Jones, 27.

greatly accelerated.

Summarizing this second point, we already know a lot about using oral methods with people who are literate. We just need to surface what we know and become more intentional in using it.

Finally, we must proactively experiment with new ways to be even better in communicating with secondary oral learners. One such experiment is being done in Orlando, Florida, by Campus Crusade for Christ. A group of Christian college students are being taught how to do follow-up and discipleship using storying versus using written materials. Four types of stories are being used by the disciplers:

- God's stories (narratives from Scripture)
- Their stories (stories of the discipler's own experience with God)
- Others' stories (stories from other people's lives and video clips from movies and TV programs)
- Disciples' stories (immediate practical applications of biblical truth so that the new disciple can develop his or her own stories that can be used to minister to others, thus promoting spiritual multiplication)

Similar models are being launched with executives and professionals, as well as with new Christians in Sunday School classes.

These are but a beginning of the kinds of extensive and innovative efforts that will be necessary to learn how to use storying to connect better with secondary oral learners of all educational and socioeconomic levels. As lessons are learned, they need to be shared freely to further accelerate the learning process in how to be more effective.

We possess knowledge of the greatest story ever told. We increasingly understand how to communicate that knowledge better with the two-thirds of the population of earth who will receive it best through storying and other oral means. In recent years we have begun to see that storying can greatly increase effectiveness even with literate people, including college students and business and professional people.

Our call to action is simple: Let's do everything we can to set aside any tendencies we might have to ignore or not utilize this fact, and let's pray and take advantage of every effective method so that, in the spirit of the apostle Paul, "by all possible means we might save some."

7 a. growing engagement

A Growing Engagement

ASPECTS of the storying approach are still under development and orality is still a relatively young academic discipline. Even so, there is enough confidence in the effectiveness of oral approaches to making disciples that reputable organizations are investing resources in an ever-growing engagement of the approach. Following are several examples reflecting this growing movement.[45]

The International Mission Board (IMB) of the Southern Baptist Convention, the largest denominational international mission agency, is heavily engaged in this approach. IMB has hundreds of field teams using storying as a primary strategy in dozens of countries. In Suriname a storying strategy in one people group enabled Christianity to spread from a handful of known believers to the point of having believers living in every village in that people group in less than five years. Most villages also have a house church.

Scripture In Use (SIU) and local partners, such as Bihar Outreach Network in India and many others around the globe, have trained over 7000 grassroots workers in 50 countries in

---

45 Many of these ministries produce training and ministry resources. See the Resources section for more information about them and for contact information.

Communication Bridges to Oral Cultures. This short course equips non-Western workers to understand their own oral cultures and to develop Scripture storying skills and strategies such as storytelling-drama, cultural adaptations of Scripture in song, memorization, and recitation. SIU focuses on mentoring other agencies through the process of adopting oral methods into their missions programs in order to address orality and the needs of oral cultures within their regions of influence. In one area 75 churches have been planted with 1450 believers, in another area 30 churches were planted in two years; and in another difficult area 22 churches were planted in three years.

Over the past six years, an alliance of international agencies which has come to be known as the International Orality Network has sponsored consultations aimed at sharing insights and experiences in orality and storying and promoting the approach. Sponsoring agencies are Campus Crusade for Christ (CCC), Faith Comes by Hearing, IMB, God's Story, Progressive Vision, Scripture In Use, Wycliffe International, Southwestern Baptist Theological Seminary, and Trans World Radio (TWR).

Table 71, a partnership growing out of Amsterdam 2000, involving the leadership of CCC, Discipling A Whole Nation (DAWN), IMB, WorldTeach, Wycliffe and YWAM (Youth With A Mission), has adopted chronological Bible storying as a primary strategy of cooperative efforts.

Progressive Vision has recently produced *Following Jesus: Making Disciples of Oral Learners*, (2002) an orally-based discipleship resource. *Following Jesus* models the practice of identifying a biblical truth that should be taught, inquiring how the people group would perceive that truth through their worldview, and then selecting biblical stories that could be used to teach that truth in light of that worldview. It consists of seven modules of 53 audio CDs that teach how to communicate to oral learners. The modules give the format and tell over 400 Bible stories that enable the oral learner to go from being a new Christian to becoming a senior pastor or cross-cultural missionary without having to read.

Epic Partners International, a partnership founded by CCC,

IMB, Wycliffe and YWAM, is engaging a storying approach among unreached peoples. Epic conducts training and workshops and establishes EpiCenters around the world to enable churches or agencies to prepare forty to fifty initial stories in an unreached people's language, equipping mother-tongue storyers to tell the stories and multiply churches. It also makes audio recordings of the stories for archiving and broad sowing by volunteers.

Radio ministries are becoming increasingly involved in supporting oral approaches. FEBA Radio has partnered with other agencies in Central Asia, the Middle East and North Africa in broadcasting stories. TWR has recently identified orality as one of five top strategic initiatives.

A Deaf Bible Network has been formed fostering Deaf nationals recording Bible stories in their native sign languages: *God's Stories in Sign*. Deaf Opportunity Out Reach (DOOR) has four training sites for chronological Bible storying where Deaf leaders from over 25 countries have been trained.

Global Recordings Network (GRN, formerly Gospel Recordings) has produced audio and audio-visual Bible-based evangelism and discipling resources in more than 5500 languages designed specifically for non- and minimally-literate people groups. These resources continue to be refined as GRN develops strategic partnerships with other like-minded organizations to reach the unreached oral communicators of the world.

This growing engagement is not limited to missions agencies. Local churches are getting involved as well. Larry Johnson is a coordinator among pastors in Ellis County, Texas, a rural county south of Dallas.[46] Johnson attended a training event about oral communicators and how to work effectively with them. There he realized that there were many oral communicators in his county and came to understand how the churches could minister to them more effectively. When he returned to Ellis County, he shared his findings with pastors. "They recognized that these are the people they are not reaching through traditional churches," he said. "They may be members, but they are not in positions of

---

46   This account is provided by James B. Slack.

leadership and are probably on the fringes."

Johnson then enlisted pastors, interested educators, church members, and other skilled people to identify worldview values and beliefs among Ellis county oral communicators. They then chose biblical stories to speak to the oral peoples' view of the world, crafted them, and set about to test them through telling them to sample groups of oral people in the county. They also selected visual materials to use in conjunction with the stories. They have set a goal of planting 700 churches, most of which will meet in homes.

While making these preparations, Johnson heard through international missions announcements that leaders in Central America needed churches to partner with them in evangelizing a specific unreached people group. Today these local churches in Ellis County have gotten additional training in language and worldview issues, and have extended their use of oral strategies to Central America. Johnson comments: "We are now doing overseas among an oral people group what we have been learning to do among our own oral people in Ellis County."

Strategies using oral methods, then, are not unproven theories. They have a proven track record, beginning with biblical times and continuing to the present. Under a wide array of situations, among diverse people groups on virtually every continent, oral strategies have demonstrated their effectiveness in evangelism, discipleship, church planting, and leader development.

What can an individual do to become a part of this growing engagement in making disciples among oral learners? Here are some practical steps: Any individual reading this paper can learn more about the field of orality and storying by reading the books, visiting the websites, or contacting the agencies referenced in this paper. The individual can learn to story passages from the Bible. The individual can identify the nearby oral communicators who are not believers and look for natural opportunities to story the gospel among them and to disciple them with stories. Individuals can share their journey in storying with the local church they are part of, and investigate ways of going global like those in Ellis County have done.

Conclusions

From the time of the Gutenberg Bible, Christianity "has walked on literate feet." Christians have led the literacy movement because of desiring to read the Bible for themselves. Yet Christians increasingly are concerned that hundreds of years have passed without a comprehensive global Kingdom advance. In 2,000 years since Christ's Great Commission, only about 10% of all peoples are evangelical followers of Jesus.

Effective discipling of oral learners allows them to embrace biblical patterns of Christian life and belief and utilize communication forms that are familiar within the culture. Of necessity, discipling oral learners involves communicating the unchanging message of Scripture into varied and ever-changing cultures in worldview-sensitive ways. It means discipling in ways designed to avoid creating dependency on the discipler. It means setting the oral disciples free to evangelize, disciple, plant churches and train leaders in a never-ceasing pattern. Only then will the message be able to reach to "the uttermost parts of the earth."

So what shall we do with this fresh insight to communicate with oral learners? This is an issue for the Lausanne Committee for World Evangelization (LCWE) and the entire Christian world to investigate, embrace, propagate and utilize in finishing the task of reaching the unreached peoples of the world. Here are proposed actions:

1. The LCWE to highlight this issue as essential for the evangelization of the world, especially the unreached people groups.

2. The LCWE endorse a "Lausanne Task Force on Making Disciples of Oral Learners" to explore and implement all practical means to advance the cause of making disciples of oral learners worldwide.

3. The LCWE and others to publish material to permeate the missions world with information about oral strategies.

4. Churches and other Christian organizations to develop and implement methods, communications, and strategies such as:

   a. Local churches becoming advocates for specific unreached people groups and promoting an engagement with those people groups by using worldview-specific oral methodologies.

b. Seminaries providing curricula to train pastors and missionaries in oral methodologies.

c. Local churches around the world utilizing oral methodologies to disciple their own members as a way of avoiding syncretism.

d. Mission agencies developing strategies for their missionaries and partners to use among oral learners.

e. Regional networks hosting conferences in strategic locations around the world for awareness building about oral methodologies.

f. Regional partnerships and agencies providing training in strategic locations to train local leaders and missionaries in implementing oral strategies among the unreached.

g. Regional partnerships and agencies developing a network of trainers to train other trainers in oral methodologies.

h. Churches and agencies recording and distributing Bible stories for evangelization, discipling, and leader training.

i. Broadcast networks and agencies broadcasting chronological Bible stories and recordings of a discipleship group in a house church setting, including dialogue reflecting culturally appropriate ways of processing the story and interacting with it.

j. Funding organizations making resources available for oral methodologies to be implemented with the thousands of language groups, people groups, and segments of societies that are still unreached.

With the insights gleaned from research and collaboration, Christians have the opportunity to reach in our generation the billions of unreached people in the world headed to a Christless eternity. Following the example of Jesus' own witness through parables and proverbs, we can communicate the gospel orally in a way that these unreached people can understand, respond to, and reproduce. Let us therefore go forth embracing oral communicators as partners—together making disciples of all peoples to the glory of God!

participants
and contributors to this paper

Convener: Avery Willis, USA
Co-convener: Steve Evans, South Asia
Facilitator: Mark Snowden, USA

Victor Anderson . . . . Horn of Africa
Nils Becker . . . . USA
Jim Bowman . . . . USA
Graydon Colville, ... Australia
Steve Douglass . . . . USA
Ron Green . . . . USA
Annette Hall . . . . North Africa
Morgan Jackson . . . . USA
Andrew Kanu . . . . Sierra Leone
Derek Knell . . . . Cyprus
Grant Lovejoy . . . . USA
Durk Meijer . . . . USA
Jay Moon . . . . West Africa
Ted Olsen . . . . USA
David Payne . . . . USA
Roy Peterson . . . . USA
Sheila Ponraj . . . . India
Chandan Sah . . . . India
Vesta Sauter . . . . Hungary
David Sills . . . . USA
Jim Slack . . . . USA
Stephen Stringer . . . . West Africa
Tom Tatlow . . . . USA
LaNette Thompson . . . . West Africa
Bob Varney . . . . USA

72

glossary
for making disciples
of oral learners

THESE terms and definitions have been gathered from a variety of sources. This is not an exhaustive list and the definitions are not necessarily universally agreed upon. This is a work in progress. Some definitions will be revised after knowledgeable people continue to make suggestions. The terms below are part of the larger discussion about "making disciples of oral learners."

aliteracy A lack of interest in or enjoyment of reading; characteristic of people who are capable of reading with understanding but do not often read for pleasure. See 'post-literate'.

barriers The aspects of a culture, circumstances, or religion that hinder a listener in hearing, understanding, or acting upon the message of the Gospel. These are the 'stumbling blocks'. Barriers are discerned by studying the worldview. Barriers are beliefs, practices, or experiences that might keep unbelievers from understanding or accepting spiritual truths. Prior experiences, such as with nominal Christians, may also pose barriers. See 'bridges'.

basic Bible truths Those biblical truths which are the foundation or essence of truth leading to salvation, the New Testament Church, the discipled life and Christian leadership. The actual body of truths as expressed may vary somewhat for each worldview situation according to prior knowledge and belief. The three terms 'essential Bible Truths', 'Basic Bible Truths' and 'Universal Bible Truths' all describe the generic or basic truths needed for one of the core objectives such as evangelism, congregationalizing a people (or planting a church), discipling, leader training, etc. See 'essential Bible truths', 'universal Bible truths'.

Bible panorama   A selection of stories from the Old and New Testaments. A panorama gives a relatively fast opportunity to tell the Old Testament stories, which provide background and a foundation, as well as the New Testament stories. Alternate term for 'mini Bible' or 'panoramic Bible'. See 'fast-tracking', 'mini Bible, 'panoramic Bible'.

Bible storying   A generic term which includes the many forms of telling Bible stories, of which Chronological Bible Storying is the main format. Single stories related to ministry needs, thematic story clusters in teaching and preaching, and even storying which begins with the story of Jesus are sometimes used, according to need and strategy.

Bibleless people group   A language group or ethnic group which does not yet possess a translation of the Bible, especially the New Testament scriptures.

bridges   The beliefs, practices, or experiences of a culture that can have a beneficial influence upon a person's consideration of the gospel. God-given opportunities for witness, in which needs felt within the culture are met by the Christian faith. Bridges are discerned by studying the 'worldview'. Bridges often provide openings for heightened interest and greater relevancy of the biblical message to a person's worldview. The storyer can intentionally target issues deemed significant to the listener.

CBS   See 'Chronological Bible Storying' (acronym)

chirographic   Pertaining to a writing culture.

chronological   Arranged in the order that things happened in time.

Chronological Bible Storying (CBS)   A method of sharing biblical truths by telling the stories of the Bible as intact stories in the order that they happened in time. The person using this method leads the hearers to discover the truths in the stories for the purpose of evangelization, discipleship, church planting, and leader training. Jim Slack and J. O. Terry developed CBS when they saw the need for a purely oral approach to oral peoples. They coined the term 'storying' to differentiate CBS from Chronological Bible Teaching (see below). CBS is promoted globally by the IMB (the International Mission Board of the Southern Baptist Convention).

Chronological Bible Storytelling The act of presenting biblical truth generally in story format though the story may be deeply paraphrased or may be interrupted for teaching whenever some important issue occurs in the passage. The story may or may not be kept intact as a story. It follows a chronologically organized timeline.

Chronological Bible Teaching The type of chronological Bible instruction used by New Tribes Mission, popularized by Trevor McIlwain in the 1970s. It references biblical stories but does not necessarily tell them as intact stories. It uses exposition and explanation as teaching approaches. This presupposes at least semi-literacy on the part of the teacher. CBT methodology reflects NTM's mission of literacy development in conjunction with translation, evangelism, and church planting. See 'New Tribes Mission' and http://www.ntm.org.

church planting movement A rapidly-multiplying increase of indigenous churches planting churches with a given people group or population segment. A church planting movement is not simply an increase in the number of churches, even though this also is positive. A church planting movement occurs when the vision of churches planting churches spreads from the missionary and professional church planter into the churches themselves, so that by their very nature they are winning the lost and reproducing themselves.

communication The process of giving and understanding a message.

communication preference The preferred style or method of communication for an individual or group of people. There are two dominant poles in a communication preference continuum—oral and literate. There are major differences between literate or print-oriented communicators and oral communicators in the way they receive information. See 'literate communicator' and 'oral communicator'.

context ...the whole cognitive environment of the speaker and addressee: their worldview(s), their culture(s), the situation in which they are communicating, their conventions of communication, the immediate context of what they have already said, and any other shared information.

core story, core story list Core stories are those biblical stories which are so essential to the biblical message and/or so consistently relevant in a variety of cultures that they have been chosen again and again as missionaries put together worldview-specific story sets. A core story list, then, is descriptive rather than prescriptive; it acknowledges the stories that have been used most often in evangelism story sets. It is not intended as a 'universal' list that must always be used, but rather it provides an opportunity to see what other storyers have done. (Initially, the core story list reflected the basic list of stories which included and taught the basic truths leading to evangelism, church planting, discipling, or leader training. The most popular list is that for evangelism.) See 'training story set'.

crafting a story, story crafting Crafting Bible stories is shaping the stories from a literature format to an oral format and making such changes as needed to maintain a clear focus on the story's main point(s), to give clarity in telling, and to make necessary changes needed for accommodating certain worldview issues and story continuity leading to the storying track objective of evangelism, discipling, leader training, etc. "Crafting Bible Stories for Telling", an unpublished booklet by J. O. Terry, is available in e-format from: biblestorying@sbcglobal.net.

discovery question A question that leads the people to draw a conclusion and discover a biblical truth based on events that occur in a story. Compare 'factual question'.

discovery time The period after the story when the storyer fixes the story in the people's minds by asking someone from the group to retell the story. The storyer then leads the people to discover biblical truths by asking questions about the story.

door opener A kind of 'bridge' involving differences which appeal to the audience. Door openers appeal to people and encourage them to open their hearts and minds to hear the message. For example, Joseph forgave his brothers; this is a new value to people who emphasize honor through vengeance. They are also impressed that God was working in Joseph's life to bring good out of the bad things his brothers did; this is a new concept of God for some people. This appeals to them and opens the door to hear more of the Word. See 'bridges'.

embedded truth Truth that is embedded, retained, situated in, related to, the story and which is evident to the listener without the need to extract the truth in order for the listeners to be aware of its presence and to catch its implication for them. See 'extracted truth'.

engagement/engaged A people group is engaged when a church planting strategy, consistent with evangelical faith and practice, is under implementation. (In this respect, a people group is not engaged when it has been merely adopted, is the object of focused prayer, or is part of an advocacy strategy.)

Epic, Epic Partners International A partnership managed by IMB, YWAM, Wycliffe, Campus Crusade and Trans World Radio. The aim of this partnership is to provide new strategies and resources that will enable the Church to use Chronological Bible Storying as a primary means of reaching the remaining unreached people groups of the world. The vision of Epic is to help reach the remaining unreached people groups with the gospel in the way that best communicates to them. For most, this will require an oral approach. "The ultimate goal is to provide the entire counsel of God in the heart language of every person in a distribution format accessible to all" (from Epic Vision and Priorities document.) An initial outcome of the partnering effort is a three part introductory set of chronological Bible stories, forty to fifty stories, aimed at supporting initial indigenous-led and reproducing churches. There is no standard story set being promoted. Rather the particular set of stories varies for each people group — a redemptive panorama selected and crafted to best interact with the worldview of each group. This includes stories from the Old Testament, the Gospels, and Acts and the Epistles. See http://www.epicpartnersinternational.com.

EpiCenter Resource hub in a strategic location close to population concentration of unreached people groups. Epicenters will provide materials and training for Bible storying. Epicenters will also prepare, duplicate, and distribute recordings and written documents. Part of the Epic strategy.

Epic Quest A two-year internship program specifically devoted to Bible storying for an unreached people group. Entrance to Epic Quest is through Wycliffe, YWAM, Campus Crusade, or the IMB (including the Journeyman/ISC program). An Epic program.

Epic Venture Cooperative project of one year or less in which some short-term helpers come alongside a team in a long-term assignment specifically to further the chronological Bible storying approach. An Epic program.

essential Bible truths Biblical concepts or teachings that are applicable to all Christians, in all cultures. The biblical 'givens' that must be communicated in ministry because without them Christianity loses its distinctiveness. Sometimes referred to as biblical principles. See 'basic Bible truths', 'universal Bible truths', 'core story'.

ethnography A description of a culture. A description of the behavior and lifestyle of a people—a community, society, or ethnic group. The aim in ethnography is to understand another way of life from the 'insider's' point of view. Rather than studying people, ethnography means learning from people. An enquiry into the culture, life, and lifestyles of a specific ethnolinguistic people group. A traditional term for 'worldview'.

evangelical An evangelical Christian is a person who believes that Jesus Christ is the sole source of salvation through faith in Him, has personal faith and conversion with regeneration by the Holy Spirit, recognizes the inspired word of God as the only basis for faith and Christian living, and is committed to biblical preaching and evangelism that brings others to faith in Jesus Christ. Therefore, an evangelical church is a church that is characterized by these same beliefs and principles. Some churches that are not considered evangelical in faith and practice may contain members who are evangelical.

evangelism track The first set of stories, taught for the purpose of sharing the gospel with unbelievers or giving believers a firm foundation in God's Word.

extracted truth Truth that is extracted, that is, drawn out of a story and presented as a list of facts, issues, propositions which comprise the essence of the story. Compare 'embedded truth'.

factual question A question that can be answered from events that happened in the story without much, if any, interpretive insight. Deals with who, what, when, and where. Compare 'discovery question'.

fast-tracking The act of telling many biblical stories one after another at a single occasion with little or no opportunity given for discussion of the stories. Used to give a panorama of the biblical story, to test for receptivity, and to give witness when there is a limited window for contact, among other reasons. Formerly called 'mainstreaming'. See 'Bible panorama'.

functional illiterate / (functional illiteracy) UNESCO has recommended the following definition: "A person is <u>functionally illiterate</u> who cannot engage in all those activities in which literacy is required for effective functioning of his group and community and also for enabling him to continue to use reading, writing and calculation for his own and the community's development." A person who has had some education but does not meet a minimum standard of literacy. To read poorly and without adequate understanding. Lacks sufficient skills in literacy to function as a literate person in his or her society. Some say that statistics indicate that 70% of the world's population who are either illiterate or functionally illiterate. Please see 'illiterate' for comment on usage.

gaps The difference between potential availability of Scripture and real availability. Language, culture and other barriers and obstacles create a gap between potential and real availability. There are at least four gaps: the translation gap; the distribution gap; the literacy gap; the oral gap. The translation gap includes at least the 2,700 languages with no translation in process and the many languages waiting for Old Testament translation. The distribution gap includes the difference between the number of speakers of languages where a translation has been done and the number of copies of the text which have been printed and distributed. In some major languages there are many more speakers than there are Bibles or New Testaments distributed. The literacy gap exists where a written translated text is available, but speakers of the language are unable to read it. The oral gap exists where there is a translated text, but speakers cannot or will not learn to read it. For such people, audio, video, and radio are possible avenues to access, as well as storytelling.

grass roots evangelism Evangelism at the grassroots level; done by local believers among local believers. Indigenous evangelism resulting in local believers in indigenous churches.

grass roots church planting Church planting at the grassroots level; done by local church planters among local believers using reproducible methodology resulting in indigenous local churches.

Gutenberg Galaxy Term coined by Marshall McLuhan in his book by that name. The time, events and people in history when oral communication styles began to move toward literate communication styles in the West. The 'Gutenberg Galaxy', named for Johannes Gutenberg (renowned as the inventor of printing), is the universe of all printed books ever published. One hypothesis is that a post-Gutenberg universe is emerging based on electronic media.

heart language See 'mother tongue'.

illiterate Not able to read and write. That person is illiterate who, in a language that he speaks, cannot read and understand anything he would have understood if it had been spoken to him; and who cannot write anything that he can say. Note: Because the word 'illiterate' tends to be accompanied by negative connotations, an alternative term to consider using is 'non-literate'. See 'functional' and 'oral preference'.

IMB / International Mission Board of the Southern Baptist Convention. The International Mission Board is an entity of the Southern Baptist Convention, the nation's largest evangelical denomination, which consists of more than 40,000 churches with nearly 16 million members. The IMB's main objective is to present the gospel of Jesus Christ in order to lead individuals to saving faith in Him and resulting in church-planting movements among all the peoples of the world. IMB is one entrance into the Epic Quest program. Specifically, see http://imb.org. More generally, see http://www.sbc.net/.

intact narrative Uninterrupted story which is presented as a whole except for a possible aside or two in the story explaining something unfamiliar to the listeners. Compare 'interrupted narrative' and 'interpreted narrative'.

interpreted narrative The story which is explained, or interpreted, without telling the story. It is talking about the story, telling what is in the story, but never telling the story. Compare 'intact narrative' and 'interrupted narrative'.

interrupted narrative Telling the story and stopping, periodically, to teach, emphasizing themes and issues which occur in the story, then continuing the story until another teaching point is reached. Compare 'intact narrative' and 'interpreted narrative'.

key terms / key biblical terms A set of basic biblical vocabulary which includes the words for 'God', 'sin', 'punishment', 'sacrifice', 'reconciliation', 'promise', 'Savior' and more. There are not words for these biblical terms in all languages, or there may be words in some languages which could be used but which might carry meanings which will not accurately convey the biblical sense. Determining key terms is an important component of Bible translation.

learning preference A learning preference is the most common, comfortable and natural way that an individual receives and communicates information. Literate and oral are the two learning preferences discussed in relation to storying. Compare 'communication preference'.

linking Linking provides connectedness between stories. Carefully spanning time (spacers) and generations (place markers) so that the people know that events happened, but do not have the full details, so that the emotional investment in characters is not lost and the storyer can return to that spot in the future and provide additional stories to fill out the biblical chronology.

listening task A fact or truth that the storyer asks the people to listen for in a story.

literate That person is literate who, in a language that he speaks, can read and understand anything he would have understood if it had been spoken to him; and who can write, so that it can be read, anything that he can say.

literate communicator One whose preferred or most effective communication or learning method is in accordance with literate formats. Literate format or style expresses itself through analytic, sequential, linear, and logical thought patterns. Most missionaries are literate communicators, trying to reach oral communicators. See 'oral communicator'.

Lives of the Prophets and Lives of the Apostles A series of booklets prepared for use in the '10/40 Window' consisting of translated biblical passages which present stories of biblical characters and introduce biblical themes. These have been dramatized for audio media and radio broadcast as well.

Lomé 'Y' The Y-shaped diagram which depicts the planning process by which a storyer selects and prepares a set of stories for use in ministry, while keeping in mind the dual concerns of faithfulness to the Bible and meaningfulness to the specific worldview. Named after the place where this was first developed: Lomé, Togo. See 'Ten Step Process' for a later planning model.

mainstreaming Storying the Bible without discussion. Used to give an overview or when presentation time is limited. The storyer simply goes from story to story with appropriate linking and bridging comments and stories. More recently this term has been replaced by 'fast-tracking' in IMB usage. See 'fast-tracking'.

mini-Bible A selection of portions from the Old and New Testaments chosen to fit the context and needs of the receptor-language community. Analogous to 'story set' or 'storying track' and 'Bible panorama' or 'panoramic Bible'.

mother tongue A person's first language; the language of the hearth and home; a person's heart language; the language a person understands best; the language of fear, grief, joy, love, devotion and intimacy; the cherished language learned in infancy between mother and child.

multi-media 'Multi-media' more commonly refers to a combination of text, graphics, pictures, sound, etc. See 'aliteracy', 'post-literate' and 'secondary oral communicators'.

New Tribes Mission NTM is a missionary organization that plants churches in tribal communities to reach people who have never had opportunity to hear the gospel. NTM employs a method of Bible instruction called 'Chronological Bible Teaching'. See www.ntm.org.

non-literate An alternative term for 'illiterate'. See 'illiterate'.

non-print media Audio and videocassette tapes, disks, film, VCD, DVD, etc. Communications media other than print.

oral Bible There is no definitive oral Bible. The working definition of oral Bible is: 'The accumulated Bible stories that have been told to an oral society.' Typically, this is between 50 and 225 stories. These are usually told in chronological order, though not always, since many times specific problems, concerns, fears etc. may need to be addressed first. So an oral Bible may differ to some extent from one culture to another, depending on felt and/or actual needs, worldview, theology and so forth. Those stories which form the cornerstone of Christian faith will be represented in virtually all oral Bible collections. An oral Bible is the accumulated Bible stories that have been storied to an oral communicator or that can be recalled by memory. "For many oral communicators the only Bible they will have and effectively use is the one they have in their heads and hearts. It is this Bible, an 'oral Bible', that enables them to meditate upon God's Word in their quiet times and devotionals and use it in evangelism, discipleship, church planting, and leadership development. This oral Bible can go where many times the written Bible cannot go. It can cross borders, enter prisons... An oral Bible becomes the permanent possession of an oral communicator and is available for use at all times. Oral communicators are able to retain, recall, and repeat from memory their oral Bible."

oral Bible network A network of organizations which are all interested in proclaiming the Scriptures through oral methods. Some members are: Campus Crusade for Christ, DAWN, FCBH, Feba Radio, IMB, Global/Network, Gospel Recordings, the JESUS Film Project, New Tribes Mission, Scriptures In Use, Trans World Radio, Vernacular Media Services of JAARS, Wycliffe, and YWAM.

oral communicator Someone who prefers to learn or process information by oral rather than written means. (Thus, there are literate people whose preferred communication style is oral rather than literate, even though they can read.) Also, someone who cannot read or write. Someone whose preferred or most effective communication and learning format, style, or method is in accordance with oral formats, as contrasted to literate formats.

oral preference A preference for receiving and processing information in an oral format rather than print. That person may or may not be a reader. See 'oral communicator'.

orality Almost two-thirds of the world's population is illiterate (non-literate, preliterate) or has an oral preference (can't, won't or don't read and write.) The quality or state of being oral. The constellation of characteristics (cognitive, communicational, and relational) that are typical of cultures that function orally. See http://www. chronologicalbiblestorying.com/MANUAL/section x.htm for "109 Characteristics of Oral and Literate Communicators".

oral story models Sets of stories which are determined and agreed upon during a training session and later used by those being trained without having been written down. The outcome, primarily, of story training sessions with oral leaders. Stories are selected through study and suggestion of the trainer and the intuition of those being trained. Critical teaching truths and issues related to understanding and acceptance of the stories is discussed during the training.

oral tradition Oral traditions are unwritten sources couched in a form suitable for oral transmission. Their preservation depends upon the powers of memory of successive generations of human beings. Oral traditions consist of verbal testimonies which are repeatedly-reported statements, either spoken or sung, concerning the past. Oral tradition is a memory of memories in the most literal way, since the message is learned from what another person recalled and told. "Whenever an African bushman dies, a whole [oral] library goes out of existence." See http://www.chronologicalbiblestorying.com/ MANUAL/section x.htm for "109 Characteristics of Oral and Literate Communicators".

panoramic Bible Alternate term for 'mini Bible' or 'Bible panorama'.

people group A significantly large grouping of individuals who perceive themselves to have a common affinity for one another because of their shared language, religion, ethnicity, residence, occupation, class or caste, situation, etc. or combinations of these. For evangelistic purposes: The largest group within which the gospel can spread as a church-planting movement without encountering barriers of understanding or acceptance.

phase There are phases in the church-planting and evangelism effort, for example, a Church Planting Phase and a Church Strengthening Phase. In CBS, 'storying tracks' are utilized within phases. Within the Church Planting phase there are typically five tracks: Evangelism, Discipleship, Church Planting, Characterization, and The End Times. Within the Church Strengthening Phase there are an indefinite number of tracks, addressing maturing believers, corrective and instructive themes, church leader training, and other topics, like preaching tracks. See 'story set' and 'storying track'.

point-of-ministry storying See 'situational storying'.

post-literate At the close of the 20th century, the phenomenon in which even those who can read and write well are not doing so. The epoch of the audio-visual, termed by some 'the Multi-Media Era', has set in. Some writers also use the term 'aliteracy' to describe this phenomenon. See 'aliteracy', 'multi media,' and 'secondary oral communicators'.

post-story dialog The teaching/learning time following the told Bible story when a story is retold by listeners, listening tasks are reviewed, or discovery questions and comments are made to draw out and relate story truths to listeners' lives.

pre-evangelism The process of preparing unbelievers to hear the gospel. This involves choosing a location to hold the storying sessions, building relationships and investigating the people's worldview. This may include the telling of a few topical Bible stories to generate interest in the audience for the evangelism set of stories, such as water stories told during a well drilling project, or grief stories for the bereaved, etc.

pre-story dialog A time before the Bible story is told when proper cultural greeting, review of previous stories, needed background stories or information, and sensitizing questions or comments are made to prepare listeners for the following Bible story.

primary oral culture Cultures with no knowledge at all of writing

primary orality The state of persons totally unfamiliar with writing. People who have never 'seen' a word.

receptor language   In translation, this is the language one is translating into, not from. Opposite of source language. 'Receptor' is similar to 'target'.

reproduce, reproducing, reproducible   A Christian, an indigenous church, and/or a strategy of evangelism and church planting able to multiply or affect multiplication without outside help. Self-replicating, as in 'self-supporting, self-governing, and self-replicating.'

residual orality   This describes those who have been exposed to literacy, even learned to read in school, but who retain a strong preference for learning by oral rather than literate means.

rhetoric   The art of speaking or writing effectively. Specifically, the study of principles and rules of composition formulated by critics of ancient times. Also, the skill of the effective use of speech.

Scripture In Use or Scripture Use   See SIU or SU below.

Scripture In Use   The name of an organization which specializes in training indigenous church planters in methods of Bible storytelling and other oral communications methods. See http://www.siutraining. org. In addition, please see SIU or SU below.

secondary oral communicators   People who depend on electronic audio and visual communications (multimedia). It is said that in some developing countries people are moving directly from primary orality to secondary orality without passing through an orientation to print. "So as nonprint media become available to them, they move from being primary oral societies to becoming multimedia societies, skipping the stage of literacy." See 'aliteracy', 'post-literate'.

semi-literate   Able to read and write on an elementary level, especially when working with familiar documents and familiar ideas. Able to read but poor in communicating through writing. Students in 10th grade are often characterized as semi-literate, especially if the quality of their schooling is inadequate. If the educational system utilizes rote memory as the dominant approach to learning, even high school graduates may test out at semi-literate functionality. This is also true of some high school graduates who spend their final years in a vocational/technical training curriculum instead of a more academic, college preparatory curriculum.

session See 'story session'.

shell story models Those model story sets which outline the basic considerations for storying to a given people group and their typical worldview with its barriers and bridges to the gospel. A list of recommended Bible stories and teaching themes are given which relate to the worldview and foundational truths of the gospel the people need to hear. The stories are not fleshed out in their entirety but are given only in a listing or outline with a scripture reference base and possibly a list of the teaching points. The user must complete or fill up the shell in his preparation of the stories in the language to be used in storying.

SIL SIL International is a faith-based organization that studies, documents and assists in developing the world's lesser-known languages. Its staff shares a Christian commitment to service, academic excellence, and professional engagement through literacy, linguistics, translation, and other disciplines. One aim of SIL is to provide access to the Scriptures in the language and format (media) that best serves the people. SIL is an organization related to Wycliffe. See http://www.sil.org.

situational storying or point-of-ministry storying The use of appropriate Bible stories (often those of Jesus' ministry) during a ministry need or opportunity. The primary reason is to lift up Jesus, followed by an invitation to hear more stories. Other story themes may be used appropriate to the ministry activity, such as The Water Stories or The Hope Stories, for disaster relief and ministry.

SIU or SU Acronym for 'Scripture in Use'. Generally, 'Scripture in use' or 'Scripture use' refers to varied methods to get the translated Scriptures into use in people's lives other than literacy. These other methods include audio and videocassette recordings, indigenous music, Scripture-in-song and Bible Storying. (SIL has a Scripture Use Coordinator on a par with the Linguistic, Literacy, and Translation Coordinators.) In addition, please see 'Scripture In Use' above. (Note: SU is also the acronym for 'Scripture Union'.)

source / source language In translation, this is the language one is translating from, not into (for example, New Testament Greek.) Opposite of receptor or target language.

story crafting See 'crafting'.

story session/storying session/session The actual time when the storyer uses the storying method. During a session the storyer participates in opening conversation, reads from the Bible, tells the story, and leads discovery (dialog) time.

story set A collection of biblical stories selected for a specific ministry purpose and usually arranged in chronological order. In an initial CBS strategy, this typically consists of an evangelism story set, discipleship story set, and church-planting story set. The evangelism story set normally contains a series of stories from the Old Testament and the gospels. Church planting story sets draw from the book of Acts. Many evangelism story sets have included 20 to 25 stories that are common to most story sets; this is considered a starting point for adding other stories that present 'bridges' and address 'barriers' specific to the worldview of each people group. The first phase sets the foundation for future phases, including evangelism, church planting, discipleship, leadership development, audio-visual products, radio ministry, and Bible translation. The long-range plan is that someone among those participating in the first phase will catch a vision to continue a longer-term work to see the growth of mature churches within that people group. A story set is the list of crafted (or prepared) stories and suggested teaching/ learning activities that compose a track. See 'storying track'.

storyer The person who uses the storying method to evangelize, disciple or strengthen the church.

storying The term 'storying' is "an attempt to make a strong statement about the value of the intact, uninterrupted Bible narrative as a valuable means of teaching God's Word leading to salvation, church planting, discipling, leader training, and various ministry activities. Storying is not limited in purpose to teaching nonliterates. It is used because it is reproducible by listeners and because the use of story helps to overcome resistance or hostility to traditional Westernized teaching. See 'Chronological Bible Storying' (CBS).

storying matrix The web or structure of stories that follows the biblical timeline. This is the initial structure given in the first telling of stories or lessons which give an essential biblical framework into which other stories and later truths may be placed.

storying scarf The Storying Scarf is a cotton scarf designed to put an inexpensive set of durable pictures representing God's Word in the hands of people who could use it to independently share God's word where missionaries cannot go. It is designed to be used in conjunction with a series of 21 chronologically-arranged Bible stories. See http:// storyingscarf.com.

storying track The entire series of stories typically arranged in chronological order which have been selected for presentation to a target population for the purpose of evangelism, discipleship or leadership training, whichever the case may be. Some names of tracks are "Evangelism Track", "Review Track", "Last Lessons", or "End Times Track". In CBS, 'storying tracks' are utilized within 'phases'. A 'storying track' is equivalent to a 'story set'. In Chronological Bible Teaching the term 'phase' is used in the same way that 'track' is used to define a set of lessons in CBS. The purpose of the track is to limit the story set to those stories which serve best to accomplish the desired teaching objective. The track is for the benefit of the storyer, but is more or less kept invisible to the listeners. For instance, the storyer does not say, 'Now we will do the Discipleship Track.' See 'story set'.

Table 71 A regular gathering of mission-agency leaders which arose from the Amsterdam 2000 conference. Table 71 has adopted a cooperative strategy centered on orality and Chronological Bible Storying.

target language See 'receptor language'.

target population / target people The group the storyer is seeking to reach. Often an 'unreached people group'. The people that have been selected to whom the storyer will story. See 'receptor'.

Ten Step Process Identifies the preparation needed to develop a Bible story set:

> *Step One:* Identify the biblical principle or truth you want to communicate; make it clear and simple. *Step Two:* Consider the worldview of the chosen people group. *Step Three:* Identify the bridges, barriers, and gaps in their worldview. *Step Four:* Select the appropriate Bible story or stories that will communicate the principle considering the worldview issues of the chosen people.

Step Five: Craft the story and plan the pre-story and the post-story dialog to emphasize the principle or truth you want to communicate. *Step Six:* Tell the story in a culturally appropriate way, which will be through narrative and perhaps also through song, dance, drama, or other means. *Step Seven:* Facilitate the dialogue with the group to help them discover the meaning and the application without your having to tell them. *Step Eight:* Help the group obey the biblical principle. *Step Nine:* Establish group accountability. *Step Ten:* Encourage the group to reproduce this by modeling the principles in their own life and then telling the stories and discipling other people.

The Seed Company (TSC) An organization devoted to partnering with nationals to plant the seed of God's word; affiliated with Wycliffe. www.theseedcompany.org.

themes Central ideas or truths found in the biblical stories

track / story track A set of stories joined together by specific themes and told for a particular purpose. That list of stories which address a strategy or teaching objective. See 'storying track'.

traditional religion and culture The indigenous religion and culture of a local people.

training story set A redemptive panorama story set that covers the basic elements of a biblical worldview. This consists of the stories found to be common to many storying projects implemented around the world in different contexts in recent years. Compare 'Bible panorama', 'core story list'.

transition story A brief story told to summarize biblical events that happened between the stories in different lessons. Sometimes called a 'linking story'.

turning point Factor which is important in decisions to follow Christ in a target or receptor population.

typographic Of or relating to a print or reading culture.

unengaged See 'engagement'.

universal Bible truths See 'basic Bible truths', core story', 'essential Bible truths'.

unreached people group / UPG More broadly, an ethnic group which does not possess a church and which does not have the presence of an indigenous Christian witness. A people, usually an ethnolinguistic group, with a historical culture, language and often a geographical place of residence where there is little or no presence of evangelical Christianity, especially in the forms of Bible, Christian gospel presentations, believers, baptisms and churches. A people group within which there is no indigenous community of believing Christians about to evangelize this people group without requiring outside (cross-cultural) assistance. A group is considered 'reached' if it has a viable, indigenous, self-reproducing church movement in its midst. More specifically, a people group in which less than 2% of the population are evangelical Christians.

visual aid A picture, simple drawing, or object that will help the people remember or understand the story. Considerations: Will some pictures confuse or offend listeners due to cultural considerations? Are contextualized pictures helpful? Will the cost limit wider use?

worldview The way a specific people view the world around them. Somewhat like wearing tinted lenses, members of a culture look through their worldview, not at it. A worldview is seldom apparent to its adherents unless it comes under question. A worldview consists of fundamental cognitive, affective, and evaluative assumptions about reality. A worldview forms the core of a culture, which guides people in how to act, think, believe, function, and relate. How people look at life and the world around them, a people's view of the world. A profile of the way people within a specified culture live, act, think, and work and relate.